NATURE TOURISM
TRANSFORMATION AND DEVELOPMENT

NATURE TOURISM
TRANSFORMATION AND DEVELOPMENT

By

Taj Rawat

Mountain Research Foundation,
Dehradun
(Uttaranchal)
(INDIA)

DISCOVERY PUBLISHING HOUSE PVT. LTD.
NEW DELHI-110 002

First Published-2009

ISBN 978-81-8356-476-2

Published by:

DISCOVERY PUBLISHING HOUSE PVT. LTD.

4831/24, Ansari Road, Prahlad Street,
Darya Ganj, New Delhi-110002 (India)
Phone: 23279245 • Fax: 91-11-23253475
E-mail: dphbooks@rediffmail.com
dphtemp@indiatimes.com

Printed at:

Sachin Printers
Delhi

PREFACE

Importance of Nature Tourism

Nature tourism is losely defined as the tourism related to beautiful wild lands, nature conservation and pristine natural lands in the world. The study of indigenous culture and social customs has added an extra importance to it. The benefits from nature tourism are passed on to local people thus playing a vital role in the economic growth and development of a particular country.

Nature tourism plays a vital role in the democratisation of society by developing human resources, creating employment opportunities and spreading wealth to rural areas where poverty and unemployment are rife. These should be given high priority to basic principles of nature-tourism, ensuring compatibility with ecological sensitivity among the people and extending benefits to surrounding communities where possible.

Nature conservation is an important aspect of eco-tourism to protect the forests and vast tracts of wilderness and use them for the purpose of trekking and exploring expeditions. Such activities in the wild create a wealth of adventure options in the hill states, which are the unique eco-tourism destinations.

It is also important for all of us to ensure the survival of vulnerable species and eco-system, huge tracts of pristine valleys which have been conserved and a large number of wildlife parks and nature reserves have been established.

Many outstanding adventure sports can be developed in the Himalayan region to attract a large number of tourists from the foreign countries, keeping in view its fragile eco-system. The great outdoor adventures can also be developed in the mountain slopes and pastures.

Himachal Pradesh is the first state in the country to protect its fragile environment, particularly, the natural areas and new forest growth is expected to cover its most of the fallen forests in the state.

Himachal's natural areas provide shelter to a wealth of mountain fauna and flora including a large number of mammals and bird species.

Nature tourism makes a vital contribution to the protection and conservation of the important nature reserves. Promoting awareness among the nature lovers and creating political pressure to conserve natural resources. Adventure tourism also provides support protect wildlife population, and habitats through job creation, influx of foreign currency and capital investment.

There are great adventure options in the Himalayan states. Most of its credit goes to wildlife sanctuaries and national wild life parks in the mountaneous regions of the country. Due to its scenic landscapes, pastures, valleys, ravines and panoramic river banks, the mountain parks have become immense attraction among the foreign nationals. The rich bio-diversity in the mountains have added extra attractions to the wildlife lovers.

Undoubtedly, Himachal is the nature's peaceful paradise and most of its natural locations are excellent destinations for adventure options in our country. We have found Jubbal-Kupped, Choor Chandani, Chaupal, Chaanshal Valley, Pyuntra Valley, Taalraa Wildlife Sanctuary, Tharoch, and famous Apple Village Maraug are some of the most beautiful examples of our outdoor adventure expeditions.

The adventure sports popular among the foreign nationals are trekking, exploring, skating, skiing, slipping over slippery pastures, hang gliding, para gliding, white water rafting, Himalayan Car Rally, flying with the balloons and night and day camping amidst the forests. From ocean to sky expeditions have been more adventurous and enjoyable. Both men and women have enjoyed such events with great rejoice.

In the last twenty years, the professors, botanists, environmentalists, businessmen and journalists all have enjoyed the nature's glorious gifts. The students are more fortunate to have done this from their own resources. So, we should encourage and support nature tourism and also participate in nature conservation activities. It is certain that the life is full of peace and enjoyment in the mountains.

With great wishes,

Colonel, Premchand Thakur,

Mountaineer and explorer

Silodi, Peontra, Shimla,

Himachal Pradesh

AUTHOR'S NOTE

As a writer and explorer, I have always been fascinated by the mountains. Whenever my life passed through the upheavals and crisis, the mountains and pastures have been an immense source of inspiration and encouragement to me. Beautiful landscapes of Peontra Valley, the Moonlit Mountains of Taalraa-Tharoch, the famous pastures of Jubbal Kupped and the Mountains of Peace in Chaanshal Valley have always inspired me to trek them again and again.

I am the most fortunate person to enjoy the four seasons in the scenic valleys and pastures of Uttranchal and Himachal Pradesh. This was the golden period in my life. In this expedition of nature exploration many people supported me. I cannot forget the support and co-operation of Captain, Netra Singh Rawat from Kothi, Devprayag who provided us accurate details and information on trekking routes and tourist places of Uttaranchal and Himachal Pradesh with main trekking points of scenic importance. I cannot forget the company of Mr. Baldev Kanwar (of Mountaineering Institute, Manali (now commandant in Home Guards), during, the snow landscape study and trekking expeditions in Kupped-Jubbal in February 1996. This was the most enjoyable adventure activity ever enjoyed by the team-mates and students of Himachal. We cannot forget the generous co-operation of Colonel Premchand Thakur, Silodi in Peontra Valley who provided us meticulous information on the most outstanding trekking routes and inspired us to visit more deep into the interiors of Western Himalaya.

I am also grateful to Captain, Dr. S.S. Bisht, IGNOU New Delhi, Nand Ram Harjet environmentalist Auli, Atma Singh Journilist and trekker, (Kumar Sain), Suresh Thakur, Tharoch Himachal Pradesh for their immediate support and co-operation in my exploration expeditions in the mountains.

At the end, I can not forget the great affection and hospitality of the parents, teachers, and students who provided me their utmost support during my educational projects in the schools and colleges of Uttaranchal and Himachal Pradesh. As a nature lover and writer, I fully hope that this book will prove a milestone for all those who love, explore and protect the nature.

With Sincere Regards,
Taj Rawat, President,
TAJ RAWAT Mountain Research Foundation,
Dehradun, Uttaranchal, India

CONTENTS

1

In Love with Nature

The earth is our common homeland and it is our moral duty to protect its eco-system by all positive means. We should protect the forests and vast wilderness all over the world to make the environment more healthy and liveable. Wild land are a home for several species of fauna an flora, therefore, we should preserve the forests and protect its wildlife. It is also necessary for us to provide clean and safe environment to the people of this planet through our combined efforts we should save it from defacing and pollution.

We, all the wise citizens of the world should enjoy the beauty of nature and establish nature conservation clubs to preserve it for a longer time. We should encourage eco-tourism and other human interest activities related to forests, wilderness, valleys, rivers and pastures.

We should educate the people and the youth through various outdoor education clubs, small nature watch clubs and seed banks should be established in the villages and towns making the people more aware about the nature conservation activities.

There should be multidisciplinary approaches to outdoor learning that include standard adventure learning methods through more creative mediums like, art, theatre, music, story making etc. It can be initiated through schools and colleges.

We should create positive approaches that provide us ample opportunities for physical, emotional, intellectual and spiritual growth amidst nature. We can make it more interesting for nature watching and exploration activities.

Development of the essentially unique experiential nature of outdoor learning i.e. camping in the wilderness, reading together amidst a forest, learn more and more good things through picnic and botanical tours in the wild. Such activities inculcates learning habits among the young learners and make them more responsible in society.

India is a land of amazing natural heritage over this earth. It has a vast wealth of rich flora and fauna. With its amazing natural beauty and rich wild life it has become a heaven for natualists, environmentalists, bilogists, ornithologists, trekkers and explorers from the world over. Western Himalayas is the most beautiful part and it and is known as Nature's Peaceful Paradise among the nature lovers. This region is popular for its unique biodiversity in the world. The wilderness management in the high mountains offers a lot of adventure opportunities to the explorers, mountaineers, trekkers and bird watchers'.

The wilderness of Chaupal, Jubbal-Kupped and Sooni Panti Shimla district of Himachal Pradesh are nature's peaceful paradise and encourage eco-tourism in the region. The lovers of nature and adventure sports have shown great interest in outdoor education and have been successful in creating their own resources to develop the eco-tourism activities in the area.

Mountains are a great source of inspiration to the lovers of nature. Those whose life is jaded and recked with the city life should move to mountains to relax and re-energise themselves, into the lap of nature. Nature healing treatment is the best remedy for those working in a disturbed environment. The city life is full of boredom and pollution and a good part of their holidays can be spent in the high mountains to enjoy outdoor activities amidst beautiful natural surroundings. It is a time when we can spend some moments of life in peace and serenity with our families of friends.

It is seen that whenever we approach to a new destination, we achieve new knowledge watching panoramic views of the area. Our life is inspired by nature and its gifts to human life. If this enjoyment and pleasure is shared with family members and friends we achieve extra happiness and energy to work afresh.

In this book, we have successfully managed to provide new adventure destinations with fresh and immaculate information.

Every chapter contains detailed information on most beautiful scenic spots, trekking routes, ideal camp sites, nature watch camps and bird watching activities. We have specified our ideas on the preservation of mountain environment and cultural heritage with some distinction. The mountains provide ample opportunities to develop new eco-tourism destinations in the natural areas with Heritage tourism. Rural tourism is also considered a integrated part of this activity.

For scholars, parents, teachers and students we have provided fresh information on picnic spots, camp sites, botanical tours, outdoor activities and other enjoyable trekking expeditions.

It is hoped that in the coming days we will provide you more enjoyable information on trekking and camping in the wilderness. All the above places which we have visited were found more impressive, adventuresome and imbibed with rich cultural heritage.

Our expeditions of trekking and exploring the mountains began in the winter of 1994 when we first trekked the most beautiful pasture Kupped wilderness in Jubbal Tehsil in Shimla district of Himachal Pradesh. This place is an ideal example of wilderness management and eco-tourism in Asia. Later on, we approached to Choordhar in 1996 in the months of May-June and again Kupped-Jubbal wilderness in the winter. In the month of August 1997, we trekked the whole Chanshal valley and gained very useful information about this amazing pasture from the Gaddis and Gujjars of the area. We spent some days in their company. We visited Chaupal in the summer of 1999 and came back without any positive result except the valuable information about local trekking routes, main picnic spots and ideal camp sites in the area. The camp sites were good for bird watching and nature watching activities.

Again in August 2000, we approached Chaupal, Khirki (natures, window) and Maraug, the best apple village of Himachal. Here, we found most beautiful scenic spots above Jhays Hills, Durla Hills, Malana Valley and Soni Paantee, some 25 km from Chaupal. There is an ideal helipad, a Kali temple and an ideal camp site at the peak of Jhaya a place above Maraug. Durla Hills are quite popular for medicinal plants as it has some varieties of aromatic plants with sweet fragramce in the air. Jhaya and Durla Hills are the most beautiful picnic spots and ideal for long stay camp life. On moving forward through bus, we passed through a beautiful serpentine road through the wilderness of Chaupal up to Nerwa. The journey through this road becomes more enjoyable and delightful when we pass through the coolness of Oak and Deodar forests. Nerwa is an evergreen town full of festivity.

We were very much pleased to see Pyuntara Valley near Nerwa, some 45 kilometer from Chaupal. The Woodville Orchards, Gatoo Orchards and Ishon Kaalee temple at the mountain top are some heavenly experiences for us. The orchard is owned by Kunwar Uday Singh a businessman from Jubbal. The Woodville Orchards in Pyuntra are a beautiful example of Wilderness and Orchards tourism in this beautiful area. K. Uday Singh has played an active role in the development and promotion of tourism in Pyuntera Valley for the past two decades. Peuntra Valley is a storehouse for medicinal herbs and trees.

After completing our journey and camplife in Taalraa and adjoining forests for somedays we stayed at Tharoch, an ancient Princely village. After enjoying trekking expeditions in and out Tharoch we proceed on back to Pyuntra valley from Pyuntra valley, we•trek toward north silodee village, Reothal temple and then to Ishon temple the highest peak in the area (11,000’). Ishon is the heaven of Chaupal and Choordhar (14,000) is called the “Roof of Chaupal”. Ishon is a suitable for rock climbing and botanical tours. It is 13 km. from Pyuntera valley and we can trek it in two days joyfully. Other beautiful peaks are Reothal 8000, Gatoo 8,500 and at the last steep ride after a difficult trekking, we approached near Ishon Peak and Dharam Shala where the Temple of Goddess Kali is established. Ishon is a heavenly place where we can enjoy camp life during winter as well as summer. From Pyuntra valley, Tharoch is 45 km.

From Nerwa, we arrived at Sainj some 35 km from Nerwa. Sainj is a small but clean village with beautiful surroundings.

We can camp here near the river bed and can approach to other directions. From Sainj we arrived at Tharoch by bus which is 10 km. from Sainj bus stop. Tharoch is the most beautiful scenic place in the area after Pyuntera. It is quite peaceful, fascinating and enjoyable place for every season (Ht. 7300'). From here, we can proceed on to Taalraa peak the highest peak in the area (10,000') and most enjoyable for trekking. Again, after enjoying some days in Tharoch and Auli, we can observe the fairs and festivals of the ancient village of the area known for their cultural heritage. The pastures of Taalraa are quite popular among the trekkers of the world. There are some 25 most beautiful natural pastures and sites in the forest land.

Tharoch is 13 km. from Sainj and Chaur Basha two kilometer from Tharoch, Moralu 6 km., Kangar and Sheela 14 kilometers respectively. After completing our camplife in Peyuntra valley, we can proceed on back to Tharoch by bus or by trekking. We can proceed on to Auli village 14 k.m. on foot from Bharanoo. This is the most beautiful trekking route. We can proceed on to famous Taalraa wilderness and wild life sanctuary. The wilderness is most enchanting, beautiful and living paradise over this earth ! It is 18 kilometer from Tharoch. Gurhad is 8 kilometer from Tharoch and from Gurhad Taalraa is 10 kilometer just as eighteen kilometer from Tharoch.

The Taalraa wilderness is quite ideal and peaceful location for camp life activities, photography and botanical studies. The pastures here are quite enjoyable for nature exploration activities.

2

Nature As a Teacher

Nature is the most precious gift of learning to the living creatures of the world. It creates several channel for the education and enjoyment of a man. Man as the most civilized creature and has developed a very close affinity with nature. Nature teaches a lot of things to a man when he faces his surroundings, forests, rivers, valleys and mountain peaks etc. As a teacher, it teaches him a lot of worldly things from the very beginnig. The man develops an emotional relationship with mother nature just after his birth. Nature is his second mother and he develops an attachment with it after his mother. In some ways, after his mother the nature looks, after the man with her blessings. Experiencing the diversities of life the man learns a lot of good things from the nature and its surroundings. He enjoys the gifts of nature with the struggles he faces in his life.

Nature as the Best School

Man is the most immediate neighbour of nature as he learns several good things from it. In the abode of nature, the man enjoys numerous outdoor activities in its premises. The nature protects him in many ways as a result he takes up good lessons from its surroundings. He enjoys the beauty of forests, rivers, lakes and mountains etc. He visits the forests, crosses the river water and rides the mountains for his adventure aspirations and enjoyment. Nature teaches many great things to man which are not taught in the schools. In this way, the nature is the best teacher for all living creatures of the world. Man is the only living being in the world to exploit its resources with its maximum. When a man passes through the forest it faces many violent animals and finds ways and means to protect himself from their attack. The man passes through the river and learns to swim to cross it, the man learns to ride the mountains and experiences the most difficult terrains of nature, as a result he learns various adventuresome skills to face the hardship of life. The adventuresome activities of man with nature are popularly known as adventure sports or outdoor adventure activities. The outdoor learning activities in the nature have become popular in our life. Now, these have become the syllabus in school books.

Don't Spoil the Nature

Those who love nature should not spoil it at all. They should protect it and should teach the people not to ruin or deface it at any cost. Those who vandalise or destroy it are the enemies of nature. We should protect and love nature by all means. For this purpose nature conservation clubs should be established in schools, colleges and the villages. The parents, teachers and students should participate in the nature conservation activities and environmental festivals *i.e.* reforestation, Van Mahotsav, Vasant Panchmi, Spring Festivals and summer festivals related to nature conservation, nature exploration and nature study campaign in the forests and pastures.

We should try to explore more and more beautiful spots and scenic places to bring to the notice of the government and the non-government organizations who are involved into their maintenance and beautification.

No garbage and filth should be left over there, as we are a civilized citizens of the earth and should collect the garbage and burn it into a sate place. The natural spots and the mountain valleys should be free from garbage and pollution and those who try to pollute it should be punished with immediate effect. This earth is our common homeland and we should keep it free from pollution. There is a great need of mass awareness compaigns to protect the wild lands all over the world. The environmental awareness campaigns are more popular in Indian schools and villages.

The people who relax into the lap of nature have no any right to pollute or destroy it. They should develop civic sense and should help in the cleanliness and protection campaigns of natural surroundings.

The educated class should take the initiation to maintain the laws of nature conservation, and protect its scenic beauty by all means. There are several training courses and conservation activities to educate the masses about nature conservation.

The trekkers and visitors should take the permission from district authorities to travel through that area. One becomes more familar with some natural places when he visits a certain areas and follow with proper rules and laws of the land. We all who love mother nature should protect it by all means.

The Countryside Landowners Association should be informed about your plan to trek through their land and request them that trekkers want to stay there for some days or months for their educational activities.

The trekkers should express their gratefulness while staying over there. The landowners should be impressed with your gentleness and disciplined life.

Rules for the Lovers of Nature

(1) Don't use invalid carriage and luggage. Keep light and handy equipment with you.

(2) Pass through the non-tidal water.

(3) You can take your pet dog with you.

(4) Fire-lighting instruments should be used very carefully so that this may not invite any mishappenings in the wild.

(5) Don't remove eggs and nests from the forests, bushes and don't harm the birds and other wild animals.

(6) Don't uproot or crush wild plants and trees. Don't spoil the wild flower plants and buds.

(7) There should be strict ban on hunting, shooting and fishing in the areas of recreation.

(8) Damaging land and removing rare plants from the wild is against the law of nature. Such activities should be banned with immediate effect. Every one should know that when we destroy nature, we destroy bio-diversity and wild lives are dependent on it. Bio-diversity provides ecosystem stability, biological production (every thing we eat) hence economic stability, medicines, housing, wood, clothing and fuel all come from forests.

(9) Don't obstruct the flow of any water course. To obstruct the natural course of water means to damage the form of earth or it may create soil crosion.

(10) Don't break through any gate hedge or fence. Before doing this, a prior permission is necessary from the owner or authority to whom it belongs.

(11) Don't leave rubbish or garbage in the wild. To damage beauty and structure of nature is a worst kind of offence. The earth is our common homeland and we should always protect it.

(12) Avoid riots, disorders and indecent conduct during your nature watching expeditions. Enjoy your every moment of life while walking along the nature.

(13) Engage yourself in organized games, camping in wilderness, enjoy skiing, skating, night camping, hang gliding or para gliding. Exploration activity is the best option.

The nature watching camps can be organised both for social as well as commercial activities and it should not harm the beauty and charm of that natural site. The nature lovers should put the pollutants into a nearby safe place into a ditch. The plastic bags and polythene bags are a harmful substance and we should use paper bags in place of plastic bags.

Seeing the importance of eco-tourism, the value of wildlife and nature studies have increased many times than before. It has played an important role in it and also an excellent step for the conservation of nature to search out valleys, ravines, wilderness and rockland and protect them with the help of aware citizens of the country.

Such campaigns for nature conservation and sustainable development have become more popular in the country. The adventure lovers and nature watch groups have come forward in Jubbal-Tumroo, Choor Chandani and Chanshal valley to protect the natural areas and maintain their pristine beauty for a longer time. For this purpose, several nature conservation and environment clubs have been established in the mountain regions with the help of International Institute of Mountain

Studies and Research, New Delhi and Global Village of India (NGOs). The students have established several such clubs i.e. Wild Flower Club, The Oak Tree Club, The Rhododendron Club, Wild Grass Club, Cone Flower Club, Wild Lilly Club, the Varbascum Longifoliam Club and the Wild Fern Club etc. Such 110 clubs are in exitence in the mountain regions where professors, lecturers, highly qualified parents and students are involved in their protection. Some 3,500 nature conservation clubs are expected to come into existence in the mountain region in the next five years.

Such clubs with their specific attempt to study a particular plant and protect it in the nature provides a very good support for nature conservation activities. This also encourages other conservation clubs to come into existence and to compete with other groups in nature conservation activities with a wider perspectives.

Protect Edible Plants

A large varieties of edible plants are found in the wilderness i.e. the roots, stems, leaves, flowers, fruits are eaten from the wild plants. But there are some other examples that the wild plants are useful for human being as these provide vegetables and medicines to many families. A particular species of Fern family is edible and is used in salad and food vegetable also. It is used in several food items among the rural and urban people. A large majority of village people surrounding the fern forests survives on it.

In many places in the mountains, several Fern Clubs have come into existence because of conservation awareness among the people. The edible fern is known as linguda (Lingad in Himachali) and is very much known among the village women from the very ancient time. The fern is cooked as vegetable and makes a perfect vegetable dish. During our Nature Watch and exploration expeditions we cooked the wild vegetable almost every day. The fern is known for its nutritious values and is eaten by villagers in the form of cooked vegetable. Rice, Rajma, and fern makes a very good combination of a delicious dish in the hills. In Himachal, Chaupal has some beautiful mountain fern forests in Khirki, Rewal Pul and Durla Hills.

During winter the boiled fern buds are made saltish and eaten as boiled salad with rice and daal. It becomes more enjoyable and delightful dish in the company of good friends. The tourists and trekkers also enjoy such dishes in local restaurants and villages.

In Nepali language, the fern is called Daunrya or neora. In Garhwali dialect it is called linguda. In Kumaoni dialect, it is called limud and lingod. Linguda is an edible fern and is considered among the most delicious wild vegetables.

"The people in the mountains use it as the most delicious vegetable dish. The linguda with daal adds a nice taste and flavour to food with chapatis. When there is scarcity of domestic vegetables, Linguda is the only option for food vegetables." Explains Ms. Kiran Tewari, a lecturer and environmentalist from New Delhi.

Secondly, in the mountain river banks **"Papadi"** (wild Arabi or Pindaloo) is considered the most delicious vegetable. It is found at the banks of small rivulets in the temperate or semi-temperate mountain valleys. It's leaves are used as the food vegetables and are among the most delicious items with chapatis. The pakoras (tempuras), Patyur, dried leaf Pakoras and other Namkeens are prepared by this vegetable. It is a very small species of Arabi (Yam) and is found near the river banks in the mountains. It is an aquatic plant and is used in multiples ways of foods in the villages. We remember good old days.

Ghanya (Ghanee): Ghanya is an alpine herb found at the height of 6000′ to 7000′. This is a medicinal herb cum food vegetable. It is found at the height of 6000 in Pauri Hills. It is used as vegetable in several villages. This herb is six to ten inch in length and provides violet flowers during July-August. The buds of these violet flowers are used in food vegetables which itself is a delicious dish. The Pakoris, Patyurs and other Namkeen items are also prepared from the buds of the flowers.

In Pauri hills, the plant is called "Ghanya", and in Himachal, it is called "Ghannee" and Ghanyar in Kumaouni language (also Ghanya). The vegetable is most popularly used in food in the Hills of Gagwarsyun Patti in Pauri Garhwal. It is found above the hills of Tamlaag, Gahar, Gagwarsyun and Kanshkhet in Paidulsyun area.

In Khatsyun, Seeku, Jaspur Kandai, Simtoli-Nagarja, Gamath and other high peaks and steep slopes. The exact hight at which it is found is 6000′-7000′. In Himachal, we have seen it in Tumroo Table Peak, Kupped wilderness (Jubbal) Chanshal Valley (Rohru), Tharoch, Chaur Basha, Bairog, Bharmana, Kangar and the areas of Chajpur wildlife sanctuary.

Orchids: Some of the orchids are tuberous and aromatic and used in food vegetable and medicines. The edible orchids are found in Bharmana, Tharoch, Moralu, Kangar, Taalraa, Jubbal-Kupped and Tumroo in Himachal Pradesh. There are so many species of orchids found in the hills.

Kathee (Asheen and Shakeen buds): A purple flowering bush known for its medicinal values and food vegetables. The branches of this multipurpose bush remain full of buds and flowers. All the flowers and buds are collected in a dry newspaper. Later on washed properly with clean water and boiled in a pressure cooker. Grinding and pasting is done properly and the paste is used in Pakoris, Paranthas, vegetables and several other Namkeen items. This is an evergreen bush but flowers in July-August. Kathee is found in Nerwa- Pyuntera valley, Ringet Kiar, Tharoch and Bharmana in Chaupal tehsil of Himachal Pradesh. It is found almost all over the temperate mountains of the Himalayas.

Badela: Badela is a delicious vegetable and is found both at the gardens as well as the moisturous valleys. The vegetable is the most delicious item and used in the dry chapatis and rice. This vegetable can be taken for dietary solutions for those who have constipation and suffering from anaemia have sufficient space for gardening in the villages.

Vanashpa (viola serpens) is known for its flavour in tea and milk and also used in medicine for liver, stomach and bileduct. This violet flower, small herb is an amazing medicine for the people who have problems of indigestion.

Kamalya: It is a flowering herb found at the moisturous places on the rocks. Its leaves are like blanket, fat, and hairy- that is why it is called “Kamalya”. Its flowers and buds are of dark purple colour and used in vegetables.

Maaloo: The flowers of Maaloo, wild Kachnar and other bushes are used in food vegetables. They are eaten raw also. The buds and flowers are used in Pakori, daal, vegetables and paranthas.

Timla (Timul). It is a large plant of ficus family and its fruits are sweetest and eaten during rainy season. The young buds and fruits are used in vegetables, paranthas, chapatis and other items.

Khaina (Khaunee) (Ficus Auriculata). This is a wild bush known for its sweetest fruits. Its young fruits are used in vegetables, paranthas and chapatis. There are several other vegetables, herbs and plants in the wild which are useful for food vegetables and medicines. The nature has provided us numerous gifts and we should use them into proper way. The nature is a mother, a teacher and protector and we all should protect it by positive means.

3

Importance of Outdoor Education

Nature provides a lot of resources to enjoy outdoor educational activities in the wild . The parents, teachers and students should enjoy their best bet by engaging themselves with several recreational activities useful to their mental and physical fitness. Such activities prepare them to re-energise and revitalise their constructive as well as innovative activities with a great practical approach. They engage themselves with other enjoyable activities of life. The man learns several good things in life from useful outdoor activities and recreational workshops in the wild during holidays. This becomes a passtime and enjoyable activity during holidays or short vacations. This brings a lot of peace and comfort to him and his family members.

It is an interesting thing to enjoy life through several delightful activities in the company of students and intelligent friends. For example, the students learn most of the unusual things in life through outdoor activities organized by the parents and teachers associations.

(1) *The outdoor games:* Several fun loving activities, full of enjoyment are organized in the wild. This includes the games and exercises for physical and mental satisfaction to the outdoor lovers.

(2) *The Creative activities:* The creative activities adds extra flavour to our life. We can get ourselves engaged in extra creative activities regularly. The open air lectures, speeches, face to face talks, competitions, paintings, exhibitions, reading together and other fun loving activities with parents, teachers and friends.

(3) *Bird Watching:* Bird watching is the one of the best recreative and pass time hobby. Bird watching is an ideal and most enjoyable recreation in the wild. Some of the mountain regions are peaceful natural resorts and are known for their beautiful landscapes. These have become popular for nature tourism, bird matching and exploration activities. There are several amazing and beautiful pastures in the wild lands of Shimla district of Himachal Pradesh. The natural areas like, Jubbal pastures, Tharoch, Saraahan, Chanshal and Kufri can be explored with the aim of eco-tourism and nature studies. One can enjoy such activites with full enjoyment and pleasure. There are several species of colourful magpies and song birds. We can continuously watch them for our pleasure. Their songs are the sweetest one in the nature.

(4) *Explore the Nature with the Hunt for Wild Flowers:* It becomes an exciting activity when the students explore valleys pastures, river banks and the ravines in the high mountains and wilderness. They search out beautiful amazing plants and exciting wild flowers with multiple colours.

There is a lot of enjoyment and recreation in the exploration of nature. Natures' gifts are always useful to man and his fellowmen. There are some examples :

1. The vast stretches of pastures
2. The lush green valleys
3. Sunsets and sunrises
4. The river banks
5. The gushing water springs
6. Sprouting Geysers in the high mountains
7. Mountain peaks, openland amid the forests.
8. Bhojpatra forests
9. Pine forests
10. Wet lands
11. Aquatic plants
12. Insectivorous plants, their physical characters
13. Oak forests
14. Cedar forests

15. Mountain Lilies
16. Terrestrial orchids
17. Mountain flowers and wild plants
    (*a*) Alpine wild flowers
    (*b*) Temperate wild flowers
    (*c*) Grassy cotton plants
    (*d*) Exploring flowering pastures
    (*e*) Valleys of flowers
    (*f*) River banks full of wild flowers and aqurtic plants.
    (*g*) Study of Moss plants (Alpine moss, foot hill moss and river bank moss plants)
    (*h*) The study of fern forests (Types of fern)

The study of flowering pastures and small forests provides more knowledge on plant study. The pastures are full of aromatic plants and medicinal herbs and provide us more knowledge on small herbs and plants. Our thirst for exploring nature and wild flowers increases continuously. We should try our best to study the plants and write about them in our regular diary.

Such activities provide us sheer delight when we pass through the mountain pastures and hunt for wild flowers for photographic work or draw a sketch out of it. The wild flowers in Pyuntera Valley, Tharoch and Chanshal Valley are most impressive and exciting. The Kupped Pastures and Chanshal Valley are the best spread pastures to explore. These are full of wildflowers, alpine plants, water sources, valleys and caves in the wild. It provides us in exciting experience of life and inspires to learn more about man and nature.

(5) *Trekking Expeditions:* Sometime the teachers of a school organise trekking expeditions among the students and a schield or cup is given to the students who performs all the good qualities of a trekker. Such activities are encouraged among students with team spirit, self confidence and nation building. Several other outdoor adventure sports activities are organised in the wilderness.

(6) *Botanical Spot Reading:* Botanical spot reading is a most enjoyable and passtime activity in the wild. Both young and old people can enjoy this activity in groups. The school students are encouraged in such activites so that they may perform well in the coming examination. They are trained to become the expert botanists in the near future

In this process, every person has to locate a plant or tree and has to explain its qualities and usefulness to the mankind. Its botanical name, family, species and sub-species etc is also explained with proper details. The ornamental and economic importance of the plants is also described by the students.

(7) *Essay Writing:* Paintings and essay writing competitions, crossword puzzles, locate the trees of your choice and lectures are organised in the wild. Other fun loving activities related to it are organised from time to time. The essay writing competitions, at the spot paintings, drawing and sketches activities are organised among school students to make it an enjoyable event.

(8) *Painting Competition:* Special painting competitions and exhibitions are organized with the cooperation of parents, teachers associations. Drawing the sketches of important personalities and landscape studies are organized in the lap of nature. The students perform well and provide a creative berth for the future activities.

(9) *Reading Activities and Discussions Among the Groups:* The group discussions, reading loudly with family members, enjoying reading together in the wild are the best fun loving activities. The discussions on new books can be organized with family members and fellow men and women. The discussion goes on the fresh novels, poetry, story and the best author of the year. Sometime, the passages of the books are discussed and the content areas of the passages are studied with comprehensive details. It becomes more enjoyable and a delightful activity as well.

Some notes on botanical spot readings. Some 30 years back botanical spot reading was a part of practical examinations in MSc. and BSc. classes but now it has taken the shape of an outdoor studies.

The parents, teachers and students visit the forest land, pastures or wilderness and find out the plants of their choice. It become quite difficult at the initial stage but it becomes an interesting hobby leter on. For example, it encourages us to search out medicinal plants in the wild and locate the plants of your choice. As it is given below:

(*a*) The types of ferns:	(*b*) The types of Orchids
1. Dragon fern	1. White horse (comb orchid)
2. Spiders fern	2. Lady's slipper
3. Edible fern	3. Purple garland
4. Ornament fern	4. Vanda Rox burghii (Rasna)
5. Single blade ferns.	5. Dendrobium macraei (Jivanti)

The Dragon fern is found in the valleys or river banks. It is a bush of 6-7 feet ht. It is found in warm and moisturous places.

The spiders fern is found above 7000 and is available at the shade loving ones or moisturous places.

The edible fern is found at the moisturous but semi-temperate areas. It is used in place of green vegetables. It is available the year round and its buds are plucked from the original plant. There are at least a dozen buds coming out of its root. The vegetable is not used during rainy season as it becomes quite harmful during that period.

(*c*) Searching out of moss plants in the nature is also an interesting hobby. The moss plant is found at the height of 3,000 to 11,000 respectively. The height of the plant is two inch long and a needle like stem and a developed capsule is there.

(*i*) The moss found at the foot hills is one inch long with a long capsule and a bunch of green leaves at the base of the plant.

(*ii*) The moss found at the temperate zones is somewhat a healthy plant with a strong stem and a large capsule at the apex of the plant. At the base of the plant there is a bunch of leaves which is of dark green colour.

(*iii*) It is quite interesting to locate the moss plants in the nature and study them in various environments.

(*d*) The orchids are the most exciting plants in the wild. It has multipurpose medicinal as well as ornamental qualities. The flowers are the most developed in the world and have unique structure. Most of the species are quite popular in the world and are known for their colour combinations.

(*e*) Mountain lilies are also most enjoyable plants in the wild. We can search out them at the height 4000-5000 (also upto 7000). There are alpine lilies and temperate zone lilies.

Jangli Piyaj (Kanda) is a popular lily of sub-Himalayan tracts of Western Himalayas, also Konkan, Coromandel Coast and Bihar. The explorers have made lily tracks in the Himalayan region to encourage botanical tourism. This is being considered a wise step by the explorers and nature watchers.

(*f*) The plants like Lisimachia punctata, varbascum longifoliam, Varbascum Thapsus, Troleus Himalayensis, Leontopodium Alpinum can also be located in the Indian mountain areas.

Peontra valley is a heaven for all these plants found in the nature. There are some beautiful colonies of ferns, lilies, orchids, moss, riccia, marcantias and other beautiful and amazing plants.

Murya (Moru) korehi jar (Cyperus rotundus) is a popular herb of Garhwal Himalayas. This is an important medicinal plants of Uttaranchal and used in stomoch pain, ulcer, cancer and blood circulation.

4

Nature As a Peaceful Paradise

The beauty and charm of nature has always been fascinated in in the minds of poets and writers world over from the very ancient times. The nature provided shelter to poets, writers and explorers with its abound natural charm and beauty. Nature is a reliable companion to man both in sorrow and happiness. It is a peaceful experience to live in or to relax into the lap of mother nature.

Several poets and writers in the world have fallen in love with nature and have explained it in the form of their greatest creations. Most of poets have described the nature as their own mother, some a beautiful companion and some a paradise on earth. The nature also has been compared with the Venus or the Goddess of Beauty on this earth.

The explorers were quite amazed when they explored the Amazonia, the largest wilderness over this earth. It is the largest wilderness in the world and a home of largest numbers of mammals, reptiles, primates, birds, insects and other strange animals. The other wilderness are in African countries, South East Asian Countries. The Antarctica is a wilderness without human population.

The Himalayas, the river valleys and ravines have been haunting the travellers mind from the very beginning of human life. The persons who know and understand the values and norms of nature is the best learner in the world. Nature teaches us several things in life which are not described into our regular lesson plans of schools and colleges. Yet, we learn several new things from the nature regularly.

Just after coming out of his mothers womb the child lands into the earth and makes himself aware with the mother nature. The process is so smooth and slow that he becomes fully conscience he get acquaintal with nature about his surrounding after a long time. After gaining mother nature when he experiences the surroundings. It provides him shelter a proper playground and several natural things to play and enjoy life.

He is amazed to see the water falls, rivers, forests, wilderness, pastures and valleys which make a beautiful sight when he explores them in his life. This brings him more closer to the nature.

We face beautiful sites of natural importance and relax into the lap of mother nature. It provides us immense charm and excitement with peculiar delight. We search out for more beautiful places of natural importance and get excited over its beauty. We all thank God for creating such a marvellous land over this earth! This inspired us to explore more natural places in Himachal with watch the nature appreciation camps in Durla Hills, Jhaya Hills, Malana-Jubbal in Chaupal, Tumroo, Kupped in Jubbal; Jangla Ansar Valley, Ghasnot pasture, Chanshal Valley in Rohru; Choor Dhar in Haripur Dhar; Tharoch, and Taalraa pastures. It is seen that when a man is in trouble, the nature provides him solace into her lap. The mother nature encourages him, caresses him, and educates him in inspiration and adventure. Mother nature is a quick healer. It can cure a person suffering from depression if he enjoys his days in the peace and solitude of the nature.

When we are trapped in limitless complications and sorrows, mother nature is the only place where we can get rid of our problems by relaxing into her lap. After spending some days in the wild pasture land and wilderness a man gets rid off his troubles and refreshes himself for his future activities of life.

There are some beautiful wild lands is Himachal where we have enjoyed our holidays with some creation and positive approach of life.

Moralu pasture is an amazing place in Tharoch, Himachal Pradesh.

We all, as the responsible citizen of this earth should protect its natural beauty and charm. At the same time, we should educate, the teachers, parents and students.

The places of most impressive sites and panoramic views, can be compared with heaven. In true sense, such places are nature's peaceful paradise. In wilderness, only a few songbirds welcome us in the silence! We require peace and serenity for our creative writing. We find perfect peace and emotional attachment with nature when we are in loneliness!

For a few minutes, when we meditate in a hut far away in the forest and we get perfect peace and relaxation which recharges us with energy and potential for further activities. In this way, nature provides us knowledge, spiritual values, sense of learning, new things from our surroundings and environment.

In the lap of mother nature, the man learns many strange things regularly and comes closer to it. Understanding the importance of nature and the role of self in the nature is a subject of great speculation!

When we pass through amazing forests, pastures, wilderness, ravines and valleys during summer, winter and rainy days we experience different kinds of environment and music which provides us a peculiar delight satisfaction. Such things are very rare in life when we face nature with heavenly encounter of beauty, charm and with great scenic importance! The music in the silence of nature has a greater importance for the lovers of nature.

During our nature watch camps and travelling experiences in Himachal, we passed through several beautiful valleys, pastures and wildlands, amazing, untouched and virgin by now! We are quite amazed to see the silent valleys, calm and quite pastures at noon and the tidal noise of the kail, ceder and pine trees in the mountains.

The famous Taalraa Peak, Moralu, Kangar and Sheela in Tharoch, Ishon and Reothal wilderness, Gaatu and Woodville Orchards and Golanu Table land with Golanu Temple are the best natural spots in the Pyuntera Valley in Nerwa sub-tehsil. Khirkee, Durla, Jhaya Hills and Malana-Jubber Valley in chaupal are the nature's peaceful paradise to encounter in real life while trekking through the mountain wilderness.

We all should enjoy the gifts of nature. The earth is our common homeland. We all should protect it from defacing and destruction. Our nature conservation activities should remain continue all over the world.

The Study of Natural Landscapes

In the past one decade, the trekkers and explorers have developed a fancy for the natural landscapes in the mountains, deserts, river pastures and green valleys. Sometimes, the explorers of beautiful landscapes remain there for weeks as they develop a fancy or attachment to that place and after enjoying their sweetest days of life come back at their work. They enjoy the nature with their best.

The study of snow landscapes is another attraction in the mountains. The Alps countries have done excellent work in snow landscape study and research. They have come out with some positive results.

During winter or rainy days when we visit the mountain lakes, rivers or pastures we face several beautiful sites with abound natural charm and scenic beauty. It becomes one of the most auspicious season for us to trek in the mountains. It becomes more festive occasion to wander in the nature for those who are fascinated by its, beauty, charm and serenity.

We face a different landscapes in different seasons. Several beautiful streams and rivers and a marvellous greenery welcomes us. The forests and pastures are lush green almost dominated with alpine carpet grass.

The pastures with sweet fragrance from scented grass and wild flowers in July - August create a different landscape. It becomes most enjoyable season during August - September and this is the best time for nature watching and to observe the growth of mountain flowers and wild plants

In winter, when the mountains are covered fully with the snowline, the natural landscape is very scenic, delightful and most enchanting. The snow cover and the whole of landscapes becomes an ideal place for the study of density of snow cover and landscape study.

Such studies were conducted by some alpine clubs and International Institute of Mountain Studies and Research (New

Delhi) in Kupped Wilderness (12,000"), Tumroo (10,000') in Jubbal, the Chanshal Valley (13,000'), Chandra Taal (17,000') in Rohru, Tharoch-Taalraa Peak, Moraloo Peak, Woodville Orchards, Ishon-Peak (10,000'), Reothal Wilderness (8,000') in Pyuntera Valley of Chaupal tehsil, are some of the best places to study snow landscapes in Himachal Pradesh.

In Uttaranchal, Nagarja (7,500') Simtoli, Seeku, Ghandiyal Khal and Bubakhal (8000') in Pauri Garhwal were found the suitable places for snowlandscape studies. During winter, the mountain peaks in the surrounding areas are fully covered with snow and are almost ready for landscape studies.

The studies related to snow landscapes have a significant impact on human life. The countries involved in snow landscape studies are Switzerland, Sweden, UK and other advanced Western countries. Switzerland has done excellent work in the snow and landscape studies.

Snow layers, snow rocks and landscapes have gained a new momentum in the snow landscape studies and research. There is a great need to initiate such research work in Himachal Pradesh to educate the people with a new dimension. Landscape studies have a large scope in the snowclad mountains in Himachal and other mountaineous provinces of the country. The International Institute of Mountain Studies and Research has taken some initiatives to encourage snow landscape studies and research related activities with the support of some Western and Indian scientists. This has given us a positive result which we expect will prove more fruitful in the near future.

This has attracted the scholars, travellers, trekkers and snow landscape lovers from the foreign countries. The snow landscape studies in Himachal Pradesh have encouraged the people from in and around with a positive impact in the areas of tourism and trekking in the country. The snow landscape study is an advanced subject in the Western Countries. India should also adopt the system with its multipurpose aims and objects.

The snow landscape in the Western Himalayas are quite distinct and different from those of other parts of the world.

There are some areas of snow clad mountains where there is a huge quantity of ancient snow, almost centuries old. The scientists can findout the possibilities for their studies and research. The geographical formation, of valleys, slopes and forests is quite different in the Himalays. The scenic landscapes are most enjoyable adventure expeditions in the state during winter.

This has multipurpose impact on the economy of the state as it encourages the people from various socio-economic background to trek and travel through the mountains. The scientists, environmentalists and experts who come to study the geographical system of the Himalayas and snow covered landscapes create a positive impact in the minds of mountaineers and trekkers with a difference. This has encouraged mountain tourism of the country.

The people from far and near come to trek the Chanshal Valley, Choor Chandani, Jubbal-Kupped Wilderness, Sooni Peeanti Wilderness, the famous Taalraa pastures and the Wild Bird Sanctuary, Sarahan in Rampur Bushahar. The Sarahan is the most enjoyable place for trekking, bird watching and night camping.

From Sarahan, We can trek to four directions according to our daywise trekking schedule. This is the most enchanting scenic place during spring season. Here is the famous Bheemakali Temple of Mahabharata fame and a lot of things to offer for great outdoor sports. There is famous Western Himalayan Bird Sanctuary in Sarahan with 144 beautiful bird fauna of the Western Himalayan origin. Famous among those are Monal Pheasant, Jajurana, Western Himalayan Tragopan and Khaleej Pheasant. Some of the birds are quite rare and beautiful. Some of them have become extinct because of the continuous degradation of habitation and global warming. Sarahan is situated at a height of 9.000 and is a heaven during summer. It is also a summer capital of former Princely State of Rampur Bushahar. This has become a most enjoyable destination among the bird watchers, trekkers, mountaineers and travellers.

5

Amazing Wildlands of Himachal

The Antarctica and Amazonia wilderness are the largest and most amazing wilderness in the world. The Arizona and the vast tracts of South African wilderness are considered the greatest wildlands known for great outdoors and adventure tourism in modern times. Canada and South Africa have advanced ahead in the areas of eco-tourism, particularly the activities on wilderness tourism. Wilderness watching and wildland protection are quite popular campaigns in some countries. Antarctica is a land of snow without human population. It has become popular for wilderness tourism.

The Famous Natural Sites and Spots

A writer has rightly called Himachal, a land of grace and divinity. The natural sites and mountain tops in Himachal, are so immense in natural beauty and charm that the people call it nature's peaceful paradise. When we reach a mountain top and find a different landscape and charm explaining its own story. Within past two decades, I have explored most of the beautiful places of Himachal that are immensely beautiful in charm and scenic importance. The activities like nature watching, wilderness watching and wildlife tourism are a main source of eco-tourism activities in this tiny state. Eco-tourism is the backbone of ecynomy in some countries of the world. Himachal is a heaven for all these activities.

Tumroo

Near Khara Pathar Tumroo is the most fascinating mountain pasture to trek and camping in the night during winter and summer days. There are many beautiful experiences of night life in the wilderness. Tumroo is an ideal camp site for summer. It is not only a table land, but a sacred beautiful mountain also with a great inspiration to human life. It is full of mountain vegetables, wild flowers and terrestrial orchids. At front side, it faces direct sun rays and semi-temperate plants and moisture loving vegetables grow over it. The back portion of it is dark, without sunrays with shaddy environment. The moisture loving plants are full with sweet smell and beautiful flowers. The moisture loving plants are quite delicate and grow over other side of mountain. We can also face some moisture loving mountain flowers and medicinal herbs. At the top of Tumroo mountain, is the temple of local Goddess "Tumroo Ki Kali". It is a well structured picnic spot and camping site. During summer days the mountain top is full of tourists and religious people to enjoy great festivity. The mountain top is full of cool breeze. The summer days are full of air waves which are most enjoyable moments in the lap of nature. The cool breeze almost strikes at every face all the time in the months of summer. Janmashtami and Shivratri festivals are most enjoyable festivals here.

Jubbal Kupped

Jubbal - Kupped is a beautiful wilderness to enjoy trekking and exploration activities Camping during winter and summer days is full of pleasure. During snowfall, all its peaks and pastures, slopes are full of snow cover and make a perfect scenic spot to enjoy camp life. The trekkers and tourists from far and near enjoy night camping at Kupped mountain top. The Western Himalayan Pheasant, Monal and other beautiful song birds are found here in the wilderness of Jubbal - Kupped. Blue bird, karaoon and red finch are found here and are a big source of recreation to bird watchers. The other birds of winter and summer chirp in the silence of valleys. The cedar forests are full of charm and beauty of nature.

Kupped is best trekking point from where we can trek the nearby mountain peaks also. It is ten kilometer from Khara Pathar through trekking which is a most beautiful natural resort in the region. Tumroo, Khara Pathar and Kupped wilderness are a great source of adventure sports in this part of Western Himalayas. The days and nights during camplife are most romantic and enjoyable in these natural resorts.

Jubbal Kupped is the most enjoyable wilderness for eco-tourism. This place is known for adventure and trekking expeditions. During snowfall, it is the most popular resort for skiing, skating and hang gliding. Jubbal-Kupped is a treasure house of botanical wealth for all those who love wild plants and aromatic herbs. We should protect and conserve these valuable plants in the nature.

(1) It is an oldest wilderness with finest examples of eco-tourism activities in the world. It is most suitable place for camp life during day and night.

(2) It is an ideal place for mountain tourism, trekking and adventure sports. There was three time more snowfall in Kupped in the winter of 1996 and on 11th Febraury of 1999 ten feet snow fall recorded at the Kupped mountain top.

(3) It is the largest Important Plant Area (IPA) and Important Bird Area for bird watchers and wildlife lovers.

(4) 110 mountain flowers, medicinal plants, aromatic herbs (some used in tea and other food items) are found here. The world famous "Vanasha" (Viola serpens) herb used in tea is found here. Vanasha (Vanashpa in Himachali) is the remedy for heart patients.

(5) The terrestrial orchids and edible wild vegetables are found here in the mountain top of Kupped. The wild plants can be conserved here for longer time for higher studies in botany. Most of the vegetables require clinical studies in the laboratory. Advance research work should be done in this regard.

(6) It is a heaven for nature lovers and explorers.

(7) It has a wide range of wild flowers, medicinal and aromatic herbs full of sweet fragrance.

(8) It's nature's peaceful paradise, can be used for long holidaying and night time camping at the top of wilderness.

(9) We can locate here both temperate and moisture, loving plants in Kupped as well as Tumroo.

(10) Eco-tourism activities can be organised here with much funfare.

(11) The popular mountain Pheasants Monal and Jaju Rana (Western Himalayan Tragopan) can be located here.

The place is a beautiful pasture and habitat for several colourful mountain birds and insects. Monal Pheasant (Lopho phorus Impejanus) and Jaju Rana (Western Himalayan Tragopan) are the most beautiful and most endangered mountain birds of Taalraa Wilderness in Tharoch, Kupped-Jubbal and Chanshal Valley pastures. Monal is the state bird of Himachal.

KHARA PATHAR

Khara Pathar is the nature's window of chaupal with beautiful surroundings. This is a resting place of formerly Jubbal State. It is 100 km. from Shimla. Situated between Tumroo and Kupped mountains, it is one of the most fascinating places in the interiors of Shimla district in Himachal Pradesh. Khara Pathar is at the height of 9000" from sea level. The highest peak of Khara Pathar is 10,000'. Tumroo is 10,500 and Kupped - Jubbal is considered more than 13,000'. From Khara Pathar, Tumroo is one kilometer and Kupped-Jubbal is 10 km by trekking. In total Kupped Peak is 20 km both ways trekking routes from Khara Pathar.

Khara Pathar is a place of immense tourist importance. It is the centre point of ancient trekking routes from where we can approach to the most enchanting mountain peaks in the surrounding areas. This includes scenic forests, pastures and wilderness. The ancient mule routes can be located just after passing through the forestlands. Khara Pathar is the most enchanting place. We can observe mountain flowers and aromatic plants in the months of August to September. The summer days are most pleasant and romantic in the surrounding of Khara Pathar. The spring flowers are in full blossom with their everlasiting fragrance.

Khara Pathar has become a perfect example of nature tourism and eco-tourism in Himachal Pradesh. This is a place from where we can face Jubbal Kupped the most beautiful wilderness in Himachal and Tumroo, a steep mountain peak which directy faces sunrays during summer and winter with semi - temperate vegetables growing on it. The other side of the mountain is inhabited with moisture loving fungies and flowering plants. Here, we can see a cunning and clever mouse without any tail ! The multicolour beautiful song birds are found here and sing beautiful songs during spring as well as winter. When the birds sing the songs the environment is most pleasant and peaceful.

We can observe the most beautiful mountain flowers, alpine plants and medicinal herbs in Kupped and Tumroo. We have seen terrestrial orchids and other edible wild vegetables in Tumroo and Kupped. The whole of Kupped is full of moisture and higher than the Tumroo. During May-August the valleys are full of mountain flowers and aromatic plants. Seasonal orchid plants are found in the valleys and moisture loving plants have some dominance in the rock cavities and tree shades. The varities of plants and their co-existence is a very amazing thing to note here. Some plants exhibit a very good tendencies of mutual existence in the nature.

CHOOR CHANDANI (CHOOR DHAR)

Choor Chandani is at the height of 13,500 from sea level. This is the most fascinating and enjoyable destination for night camping. It is some 80 Km. from Shimla to reach Haripur Dhar via Solan. Choor Chandani is the highest mountain peak of Chaupal. In winter during snowfall it provides the beautiful glimpses of moonlit nights.

The famous trekkers and lovers of nature call it moonlit paradise on earth! The whole peak shines in the moonlit nights. At day time, Choor Chandani is visible from the far away peaks. During snowfall, it becomes more pleasant and enjoyable to trek it from Nauradhar or Haripur Dhar. Choor Dhar is known for heavenly peace on earth. During summer we can trek it upto the peak through Sarai near Chaupal. The sweet fragrance of wild flowers and aromatic plants fill the environment with delight and enjoyment. The peak-top becomes a paradise to enjoy night life into the lap of mother nature. Here starts the real outdoor life of adventure lovers and those who want to enjoy nature with their every moment of delight. We come across several beautiful pastures after the visit Bijat Maharaj Temple.

Choor Dhar is an Improtant Plant Area and widely known for its wild flowers, medicinal plants and aromatic herbs. Those, who after a difficult trekking arrive first at the top. One gets semi-conscious or unconscious for a while because of sweet fragrance of aromatic plants and wild flowers. Choor Dhar is a place known for botanical tracks, tours and in many ways has great importance for higher research work on wild flowers and alpine plants. Kaalaa Baagh is the most beautiful pasture for the studies of wild flowers and medicinal herbs.

Cool breeze welcomes us here at every corner of this mountain and the wild flowers and aromatic plants swing into the air. This is an amazing and delightful movement when all the mountain flowers are swept aside by the strong air strokes. The thrust of the air with sweet fragrance of flowers fills our nostrils with delight which lingers into our memory for a longer time.

Choor-Chandani is a place where we can rejoice in camplife amidst the silence and peace of nature. With abound natural beauty, charm and the mountain slopes entertain us with its amazing pastures and forests amidst the sweet chirping songs of the wild birds and the buzzing noise of the honeybees.

The other trekking route to Choor Dhar is from Sanrai. Here after covering some distance, we can face Bijat Maharaj Temple, Dharmshala and other shops for food and recreation. Bijat Devta and Chooreshwar Mahadev are quite popular in the area. The pilgrims visit here to have the Darshan of Chooreshwar Mahadev and Bijat Devta. The journey almost remains fruitful to all the devotees who come here from far and near. The trekking route from Bijat Temple to choor dhar is quite difficult and arduous.

HARIPUR DHAR

Haripur Dhar is the most enchanting place, a small town from where one can approach to Choor Dhar. The summer cool breeze welcomes us at Haripur Dhar. It is a good stay point with cheap and best food available in the small Dhabas and restaurants.

Haripur Dhar, itself is a very good place for the studies of wildflowers and botanical collection. The place is quite popular for wild flower tracks and tours. The important wild flowers are: Viola serpens, Lisimachia Punctata, Trollius Himalayensis, Lilium Himalayensis, Leontopodium alpinum, Chamoenerium angustifoliam and Varbascum longifoliam type of plants. Some flowers and bushes are just like hand shaped or sometime like a garland hanging into the air. It presents a very fascination glimpse from the mountain peaks. The summer days in the surrounding of Haripur Dhar and night camps are not only full of enjoyment and adventure but provide peace of mind and re-energise us for the future activities. During summer days, the cool breeze welcomes the visitors in Haripur Dhar. One can spend some good days in Haripur Dhar as the food and stay facilities are available here.

The natural surrounding is very welcoming and romantic in summer days. It is more scenic, easy and full of natural spots with amazing beauty and charm.

We can approach to Haripur Dhar through Shillai in Sirmaur via Rajgarh from Solan district. It is a very enjoyable journey by bus upto Haripur Dhar and adventuresome by trekking from Haripur Dhar Base camp to Choor Chandani pasture. "The surroundings and heavenly nature of Haripur Dhar compells us to "camp here for some days. For summer the place is the most enjoyable and peace loving", explains a well known trekker of Himachal Pradesh.

It is a peaceful paradise of nature and the summer days are most pleasant, enjoyable and peaceful while trekking up to Choor Dhar.

The visit to Haripur Dhar is most fascinating and romantic while camping in the surrounding of wildlands. During the months of summer the tourists rejoice the night life camps with fellowmates. The roadside wild flowers and alpine grasses and huge trees welcome the trekkers and visitors with their amazing characteristics. The wild flowers invite us with striking beautiful colours.

This place is a beautiful site of wild flowers colonies and creates a marvellous impression in the minds of botanists, environmentalists and mountain flora experts who come here to camp in the wild to study the wild flowers and alpine plants.

Haripur Dhar is an Important Plant Area (IPA) in many ways. The wild lands are known for the study of medicinal plants and aromatic herbs. The Vanasha (viola serpens) is a popular medicinal plant used in the flavour of milk, tea and coffee. The Traditional doctors use it as herbal medicines in the local villages.

NAURA DHAR

Naura Dhar is the most enjoyable place for peace lovers and trekkers of the country. It is most suitable place for camp site and night time enjoyment amidst the forestland. Naura Dhar becomes more enjoyable during the moonlit nights and summer days. The beautiful bushes open pastures and grassy slopes are an excellent place for ideal campsites.

Naura Dhar is normal during summer and colder during winter. The beautiful mountain flowers welcome us during April-May and August - September. We can face several species of wild flowers during winter. This is an amazing wild land to the lovers of wild flowers and collectors of alpine plants of the country. We can organise several botanical tours and can collect several important botanicals for our herbarium collections. Some environment clubs and NGOs are doing nature conservation work in Naura Dhar.

It becomes more exciting and enjoyable when we face the wild plants in the nature. The surrounding of Naura Dhar is full of wild bushes, dwarf trees, herbs, shrubs and heath lands. It is beautifully located. The trekkers route through Nauradhar goes to Choordhar which is considered a paradise for the local trekkers and explorers. It is not only a place for all seasons but a spot for every enjoyment of life through adventure skills. The night camp is much more enjoyable and the day time is more useful for trekking and photographic skills.

The forests, rocks, wild bushes and dense forest land, combined with wild ferns, moisture plants, wild flowers and alpine plants and herbs make us full of excitement when we pass through them.

Naura Dhar is famous for natures' nursery of wild plants. A variety of them is edible, medicinal and bushes can also be used in food vegetables. The bushes like toonga, jal toonga, fern, Vanaspa (viola), stonewort, lupia, and sunflowers, are found in the wild. Viola serpens and kungji - a sweet smelling herb are used in tea and milk is good for health. We all the lovers of nature should protect and enjoy such gifts of nature in the wilderness of Naura Dhar.

We can trek to Choor Chandani from the Naura Dhar in a zigzag fashion. Trekking may be very arduous and difficult but full of romance of adventure. If we have a good company of trekkers and explorers, the journey becomes more easy, lively and fruitful all the days.

Choor Chandani is the most lively and beautiful mountain peak almost covered with snow the whole winter upto summer. We face a lot of challenging routes while trekking through Naura Dhar upto Choor Dhar. When we approach to our destination, the journey becomes more romantic, lively and stimulating with various other positive activities with the fellow mates when we camp in the wild.

6

Chaupal's Beautiful Forests And Valleys

Chaupal from Shimla is situated the height of 7000′. It is 100 km, Maraug 80 km, Nerwa 135 km. respectively. The queen of hills Chaupal has best lush green pastures and alpine forests known for its beautiful landscapes and mountain slopes. During summer as well as winter it becomes more enjoyable to trek through the rivers, valleys and the forests. During winter the snow clad mountains resemble with the alpine forests of Switzerland.

Chaupal: Chaupal means a meeting place or courtyard which opens from four sides. Chaupal is naturally, a peaceful paradise on earth which is linked by trekking routes from all directions. The ancient trekking routes are quite conspicuous and well-defined in its ancient mule routes. During Jubbal State the mule routes were having big importance as no motor roads were constructed in those days. The mule treks passing through the forests with main stay points speak the story of by gone Princely era. Chaupal now is linked by bus roads and almost is linked to all the important places of Shimla district.

Chaupal is surrounded by beautiful cedar and kail forests which give an impression of Swiss Alps. The area gives an impression of wilderness which has 70% forest area in the region. Many beautiful houses and villages have settled down in the forest land which once was a wilderness in the British Raj. The orchards have replaced the old agriculture pattern and the apples and other fruit plants have taken over as the main crops. The orchards have brought prosperity to the people in Himachal. This is the fruit of the peoples hard and sustaining work for their survival. The orchardists here are richest in Shimla district.

The mountain slopes and valleys in and around Chaupal are full of greenery and almost attract the trekkers and tourists from far and near. Chaupal is also known for its wild flowers and important plant areas. The alpine bird fauna is rich in Chaupal and surrounding valleys.

From Chaupal to Maraug, we face beautiful rock structures for climbing expeditions. The rocks, steep mountain slopes and valleys in Chaupal wilderness are full of edible Fern and wild fruit plants. The forest cover in Chaupal remind Swiss Alpine forests. The magnificent view of Chaupal forests from Chambi Dhar and nearby mountain peaks is quit amazing. During snow fall the site is completely enchanting and quite commanding. The trekkers and tourists have a great fascination when they have a birds eye view of the most beautiful composition of cedar and kail trees. This forest is spread upto 830 sq. km.

Chaupal becomes most attractive during snowfall in winter. Various adventure sports are organised during snowfall by the trekkers and travel agencies all over the mountains. During summer, Chaupal is full of mountain flowers, wild sunflowers and long stalked mountain flowers are found by the road side in the forest. The road from Chaupal to Maraug is full of edible fern bushes which is used by the village people from time to time.

The road passing through the forest of Chaupal is quite peaceful and full of panoramic sites. The road between Chaupal and Nerwa is a heaven for nature lovers and those who love slow driving when passing through the dense forests. The road passing through the Dhabas river creates a beautiful site.

It speaks quite different story and always fills our mind with the nature's journey in life. The natural views from Nerwa to Chaupal are full of fascination and create a lot of impacts in our mind with nature's beautiful landscapes.

The beautiful forests and wilderness of Chaupal should be preserved for a longer time so that it may attract the people from far and near.

The wilderness of Chaupal has a new growth of plants and is the most spectacular in the sense of wilderness watching, nature watching and nature conservation activities. It resembles by all means with Swiss Alps and during snow fall it becomes alive like Swiss Alps. The people of Chaupal should protect its surroundings and keep it pollutionless for the near future.

KHIRKI—THE WINDOW OF CHAUPAL

Khirki is a narrow neck of mountains through which a road passes to Chaupal and another road enters to Maraug through a beautiful forest track. Khirki is also called the window of Chaupal and through it we can overlook to the valleys and beautiful wilderness of Chaupal. Khirki is a passtime picnic spot and trekking point through which we can trek during holidays. Exploration and camping activities can also be done here for school children. Here, we can have tea, food and refreshment in a small roadside restaurant.

Khirki is a very small picnic spot some 25 km from Chaupal. From Khirki, the Chaupal road bifurcates, one way to theog and another for Maraug, the richest apple village of the world. From Khirki to Maraug, the road is cool, beautiful and full of alpine trees and plants. The cedar and kail trees dominate here. The rock-structure from Khirki to Maraug is very fascinating and challenging. The rock climbing camps can be organised near Khriki and Rewal Pul. Though, it is not very developed place, only one tea shop is here in the name of relaxation point but it has a lot of good locations to visit in the summer as well as winter holidays. The camps can be organised in Khirki itself, Durla wilderness and Malana Valley are at some 6 km. distance from Khirki. Khirki is nature's window of Chaupal and from here we can locate ideal campsites above the mountain pasture.

The Gujjars have temporary shelters in the nearby forests and survive on selling milk to local shop keepers. Maraug is 15 km from Khirki with beautiful amazing rocks and forest in between. The place is ideal for rock climbing and film shooting locations. Also, a very good place for summer holiday camping in the forests. The wildlife and bird fauna is found here with its common species of wildfowl, cheer pheasant, khaleej pheasant, brown horn bill and several other song birds. The mountain tiger, bear, wild fox, diamond back snake is found here.

We can locate, many beautiful places of natural importance from Khirki if the weather is clear. Khirki is at an enjoyable distance from Chaupal. The road is good and the forest life is full of peace and serenity in the morning time.

Here, we can locate ideal campsites in Lankdabeer Dhar, Reunee Dhar and Chambee Dhar. Roadsides tea shops and small restaurants are popular for trekking and small time stop over during nature exploration in the months of May upto September. Spring time is the most enjoyable for trekking and nightlife camping. Khirki is 80 km. from Shimla facing several beautiful places and natural spots in between. One should come here during summer days to enjoy the peace, serenity and romance of nature. Beautiful birds like koel, kafoo, Hanshod and several other beautiful song birds entertain us with their most enjoyable songs in the lap of mother nature.

DHURLA: THE ENCHANTING MOUNTAINS

"Durla" or Dhurla" both the names are correct in the langugge of local villagers. The villagers call it Dhurla and the literate class call it Durla. Durla is a small bus stop with two shops and a beautiful surrounding of farms, pastures and lush green forests. In many ways, it is a multipurpose place for adventure and camping sites in summer as well as in winter days. The newly married couples can have the perfect holidays of their golden nights in Dhurla and Malana Valley above the Jubber village in Chaupal. The place is not only peaceful and exciting but a nature's peaceful playground for travellers, trekkers and botanists also. The cool breeze and divine relief we get over the mountain peaks provide us immense peace and comfort, serenity and excitement in the environment of Dhurla.

Dhurla is known for the famous government potato farms where various breeds of improved variety of potatoes are grown in a big farmland. The famous potato breeds are grown here in large quantity and sent to other parts of the country. It is an established fact that Himachal is known for apple orchards and potato farms. Also, it grows off season vegetables in large quantity to meet the demands of other states.

It is an ideal camping site for summer as well as winter. There are two small shops in Durla for tea and refreshment. In winter the shops are closed down as the excessive winter climate persists here for the rest of the time. The shopkeepers settles down in the villages for the whole of winter. The summer days are most pleasant and romantic in Dhurla pastures.

During winter the Gujjars settle down to the warmer places of plains or valleys.

It is very fascinating place, for the road is parallel to the Maraug town and is enjoyable on trekking for winter as well as summer. The Durla hills are an ideal place for camping site. From the mountain tops, we can view many important peaks of the area which create a beautiful impression on the minds of visitors. We can take some good photographs by our camera and can see beautiful peaks by our telescope.

Near Dhurla, there is most fascinating place called Malana Valley. The Valley is dominated by Kail trees, creepers thorny bushes and medicinal plants. There are ten types of medicinal plants, purely aromatic. There are several other medicinal herbs which deserve clinical tests in the laboratory for their confirmation of a particular medicine. Dhurla is 25 km. from Chaupal and Chaupal is 90 km. from Shimla.

The mountain flowers like Varbascum longifoliam and lisimachia punctata are found with bright yellow flowers creating a beautiful impresson to the tourists and trekkers. Malana is the nature's peaceful paradise and when we reach at the top, we can see surrounding peaks and villages with great panoramic views.

During summer, Dhurla is a bird watchers paradise as many small and medium size birds are visible in the alpine pastures. The wildfowls, local pheasants, song birds and brown horn bills are the favourite one to spot easily. Dhurla mountains shine with golden carpet when its peaks face direct sun rays in the morning. It becomes more enjoyable scenic moment for the trekkers and explorers. When Dhurla faces red sunrays in the evening it shines like copper and gold making our mind more sensitive toward the evening effect.

The peak of Malana mountain above Jubber village is a treeless pasture. It is very nice place for camping and holidaying in the months of summer as well as winter. We can view the local peaks, Maraug and Ghareen Villages dotted with houses, orchards and woodlands. This provides us most spectacular views during rain and summer days.

Jhaya Hills: Jhaya Hills are most beautiful pastures and forests at the height of 8000'. It is combined with a Kali temple and a natural helipad at the top of the mountain peak. Through

Jhaya we can overlook the other surrounding peaks and beautiful villages dotted with orchards and woodlands. Jhaya mountain top is the most suitable example of alpine vegetation. It is an ideal spot for campsite during summer. We should definitely enjoy it during holidays.

The Maraug and Jhaya hills are the best passtime trekking spots for the camping and exploring activities. We can enjoy the blessings of mother nature here in the wilderness. Jhaya hills are quite well known for their horse neck structure and shining greenery. It becomes quite pleasant in the months of May and June. It is an ideal picnic spot at the top of Jhaya hills. It is like a helipad, a plain area for camping and other outdoor activities. The mountain top can be developed into a small airport for the purpose of domestic tourism. From Jhaya hills, we can see beautiful mountain peaks and can approach various mountain peaks of Chaupal through traditional trekking routes. The forest life remains busy and we can see various species of alpine plants and trees in the wild. The pasture of Jhaya hills have multipurpose domain of trees and plants useful to human being. Day time picnic activities and night life camping at Jhaya are some of the most enjoyable events of life. One can relax into the lap of nature with perfect ease and peace. An excessive rain may hamper your efforts of trekking or camping in the hills.

For this purpose, camp site should be located at an ideal and safe place where excessive rain or rain storms can be avoided with better camping management. Night life becomes more enjoyable and enchanting in a peaceful environment in Jhaya hills. There is an ancient temple at the top of Jhaya hills and several ancient stories and folk tales are related to it. It becomes recreative and enjoyable when we come across with many romantic stories of the time of Princely States.

Jhaya Hills have beautiful forests, ancient trekking routes and the beautiful pastures. One should enjoy adventure exploration activities in every season. Jhaya hills shine like gold when the sun rays pass through it in the morning in summer days. It becomes a heaven in the morning calm and the grass over Jhaya hills shines like a golden carpet. It becomes a most spectacular site in the days of sunshine.

7

Maraug : The Beautiful Apple Village

It is situated at some 7000' from sea level and the Jhaya hills are at the height of 8,000'. Maraug is a most beautiful village in Chaupal Tehsil known for its most fertile apple orchards. The top orchardist families of the village want to see it developed into an international tourist village and for this reason the people are united for the purpose of development of the area.

Maraug, the richest apple village in Chaupal tehsil whose per-capita income is much more in the world. And that too from apple crop. The village in many ways has become popular in the country among trekkers, explorers, hikers and horticulturists. All the apple growing countries of the world have admired the efforts and arduous work done by villagers and orchardists of Maraug. The process of development has been initiated by the people themselves by making roads, and playgrounds through their co-operative efforts on some important occasions.

Maraug is developing as an International Tourist Village and has become trekkers paradise for the past two decades. The people from Chakrata, Uttaranchal and Shillai, Himachal have trekked the beautiful mountains of Maraug through traditional mule routes. River course bifurcates the boundaries of Himachal and Uttaranchal. The socio-ethnical life in Maraug is quite different from that of Jubbal and Chaupal. Maraug and adjoining villages have unique socio-cultural life. The Pandava Period cultural heritage exists from the very ancient time. The various temples of the past and present are found abundanty and are main sources of fares and festivals and great human inspiration. Such temples are encouraging religious tourism in this part of Shimla district. The people are involved in ethno-social and cultural activities during religious fairs and festivals.

Here, the natural landscape is quite impressive and attracts the people from far and wide. The nature lovers strive for the creative activities in life. The people enjoy life on many festive occasions. Maraug is a developing village and is known for its richest apple crops in the world. The potato and other off season vegetables are also grown in the area at commercial scale.

It is surrounded by small villages, forest patches, beautiful orchards and several panoramic mountains. Besides apple orchards the villagers grow several other mountain fruits as cash crop. The orchards, the traditional village houses, ancient temples, and landscapes have become a source of inspiration among the tourists coming from far and near.

The people do understand the language of economic development through their orchards. The orchards have brought them prosperity and peace. The educated people remain in big cities and rarely return to village life. The younger generation prefers white collar jobs in cities.

On the other hand the people have seen a dawn of prosperity through the development of their orchards in the area. For example apple and other fruits are grown with great care. Here, hard work has a great importance. Potato farming is also done with great efforts which bring immediate return to their cash crops. The apple and potato are major cash crops in the area. In Maraug and adjoining areas, there are 150 big orchardists and 560 average good growers rest 3000 local orchardists are common farmers and can survive alone on apple crops every year provided that there is no natural damage to the crop. Besides this, the farmers are more confident on their vegetable crops every year.

The younger generation is much more qualified and experienced to look after their precious orchards with more scientific ways. They are involved in growing to marketing and transportation. They are doing their great efforts in farming which brings immediate return to their cash crops. The potato farms bring them Rs. One to Five lakhs every year in Jubbal area. Some farmers earn upto Rs. ten lakhs and more from their potato crops. The apple orchards bring them from Rs. two lakhs to fourty lakhs annually in Maraug and adjoining areas. If the natural calamities do not harm them, the future is bright for the farmers of Maraug. There are some orchardists in Himachal who earn upto three crores annually.

Unfortunately, most of the crops is wasted away in enroute to the market because of improper transportation and careless storage. The mountain fruits waste away in the open fields and the people sell only 50% of their crops. A large part of nest of the crop is wasted away in the process.

Secondly, they do not get proper prices of their fruits. The brokers take the orchards on contract and sometime the orchardists are paid Rs. 20.000 instead of a price of Rs. 150,000. This is sheer expoitation of the poor orchardists. Sometime, they do not get even the prices of their labour, fertilizers and hard sustaining work done by the family members. Maraug is a model example of apple cultivation in Chaupal region and the Government should take this village as the model example for their horticulture project and studies.

In this regard the Government should think to consider about the fate of the orchardists of Himachal Pradesh and should provide a good supporting price of their crops. There is a great need of a mutual understanding between the apple marketing companies and the orchardists just to fix the proper prices for apples.

Maraug is an excellent example of an International Apple Village where per capita income is quite impressive in comparison to other apple villages of the world. The people are impressively happy and the life is full of enjoyment. They work hard and enjoy life with their best. Earlier, the people were surrounded by many superstitions and were involved in various religious and social activities. Now, their life involves in and around of their orchards. Some of them are the orchardists of international fame and have the knowledge of technical know how about the development of orchards. One such orchardist is Mr. Bhupinder Negta of Ghareen who has specialised in the management of apple orchards in most modern ways.

Development Process

Maraug is the most enchanting village situated in the lap of nature, surrounded by beautiful mountains and valleys. It can be developed into an eco-friendly tourists village in Himachal. Himachal Pradesh has already set a record in nature conservation and reforestation. It has become an ideal state to initiate environmental awareness programmes. It has set a marvellous example in eco-tourism development in the country. Chanshal valley, Tharoch and Jubbal-Kupped, wilderness are the best examples of eco-tourism distinations. Nature conservation work is going on with the best efforts of local citizens and NGOs like Global Village of India, New Delhi.

Maraug can be developed into a most scenic and multipurpose tourist village surrounded by dotted apple orchards and beautiful homesteads. The houses built within the apple orchards are full of peace, natural beauty and liveliness. The orchardists of Himachal Pradesh are very honest, intelligent, hard working, sincere and peace loving people in the world. The only thing they require is the proper supporting price and proper marketing for their apple crops. The government sources, apple merchants, transporters and orchardists should work in full co-operation. All the things are co-related in the areas of horticulture, development, national income and the survival of orchardists who work hard day and night to look after their orchards. It means they should get their proper support prices when their crop is ready. This is the price of their hard and sustaining labour.

NERWA : A CITY OF FESTIVITY

Nerwa is a bustling busy town in Chaupal Tehsil. In good old days, Nerwa was a temporary stay point for trekkers, mule herders and local visitors and traders. It had only two or three shops an ancient days and later on it was developed into a temporary residental place for the officers during Princely states. Now with the pace of time adventure some people started to settle down at Newra and it was developed into a fulfledged town in the out skirts of Chaupal. Nerwa is 35 km. from Chaupal and it has an equal distance to Rewal Pul, gateway to Maraug Valley. Presently, the population of Nerwa is above 10,000.

Nerwa during Summer: The sun is intolerable in Nerwa during summer. It is a busy town situated on the bank of Dhabas (Shalvi) river almost surrounded by rocky mountains and valleys. It remains hot during summer and colder during winter. But it is immensely an enjoyable place for winter days. Nerwa is good for holidaying during winter and the rocks are excellent for rock-climbing. The surrounding mountains and pastures are a subject for nature study. It is 35 km. from Chaupal with many enjoyable stops in between. The whole area is covered with lush green grasses in the month of July-August.

Nerwa is very hot during summer, particularly the months of May and June are difficult to stay in Nerwa. We get relief from scorching sun only when our jeep proceeds to Chaupal. Chaupal is very cold and during winter and there is heavy snowfall. It is an ideal place to enjoy life during summer days. The small restaurants are cheap and best and the life is contented and enjoyable. The cool breeze welcomes the visitors every time. The people who are habitual of cold climate, Chaupal is the most pleasant and auspicious place to enjoy life in the lap of nature.

Nerwa and the Shalwi river combine a beautiful taste to human life to enjoy swimming or river bath during summer. The local inhabitants have polluted the Shalawi river in Nerwa as they go out for call to the river. Nerwa is known for its beautiful orchards and other cold - climate mountain fruits. It has some historical importance and stories behind it. It is a warmer place in summer and colder in the winter. Nerwa the bustling town is situated on the banks of Shalwi river.

Nerwa has its outstanding beauty and natural landscapes. The people are not very aware to preserve its natural beauty and forests. The water of the river is being polluted continuously and the river banks are the worst examples of exposed pollution. It requires a lot of mass awareness to educate the people. We should create a pollutionless Nerwa.

The population of Nerwa is increasing day by day as it is becoming more congested than Chaupal. The people should think its cleanliness and beautification and traditional values and campaign for a pollution free Nerwa.

Nerwa is above 100 feet from sea level and some areas of its colonies are near the level of river banks. It is some 130 km. distance from Shimla and at the same distance from Vikas Nagar Dehradun, Uttraranchal.

The Natural Charm of "Ishon"

The name "Ishon" in the local language means the Godland or the Paradise of Gods and Goddesses. Ishon is the highest peak of Pyuntra valley and is also known as the "Crown of Pyuntra Valley" and "Heaven of Chaupal". This is the most impressive mountain peak in the area which becomes more pleasant during summer and more harsh and difficult during winter. In winter, when there is heavy snowfall (sometimes, the snowfall is three times upto January), the peak of "Ishon" is covered by 7 feet snow and the whole mountain appears into a huge beautiful Shivlingam shining with cream white snow. The whole Pyuntra valley is covered by a huge shining layer of snow as if it is a white silver carpet. The temple at the top of "Ishon" peak is fully covered with snow during winter days. It becomes more pleasant when the summer approaches and the mountain cover is dominated by green grasses, medicinal herbs and aromatic plants. During spring with from August to September the whole area is covered numerous wild flowers with sweet fragrance in the environment. During this period, the whole environment is full of enchantment, romantic prelude and the natural beauty. The romance of nature is quite amazing this time.

The Fascinating Views: We can have some most beautiful views from the mountain top of Ishon. The lush green valleys, slopy pastures, steep rocks, serpentine pedestrian paths, gushing clear water streams and forest patches remain full of natural beauty which are quite pleasent of the eyes. Here, we can observe fascinating views which impresses us from the top of the "Ishon mountain".

The Golden Fields: The golden yellow agricultural fields, the villages sites, natural surroundings and apple orchards provide us several beautiful glimpses during the clear sky. The trekkers come here to relax and enjoy in the lap of mother nature. From the mountain top of Ishon, we can see most ancient villages of Chaupal and Dhar Chandana. From here, we can view Shalan, Halau, Shatal, Kedi, Halan and several other villages full of natural beauty and rich cultural heritage. The other villages like Lohan, Paban and Bijmal are surrounded by forests and beautiful wildlands. The other beautiful villages of Pyuntra valley are Paulia, Silodi, Kedi, Pujarli, Kyarla and Tikri where some small and Big temples are in existence from the very ancient time. These villages create beautiful natural views and glimpses. The villages surrounded by cedar forests are a great source of recreation and enjoyment for trekkers, explorers and nature lovers coming from far and near.

Most Beautiful Natural Views: Pyuntra valley is known for projecting the best natural views during summer as well as winter months. The summer days remain full of bright sun and the rainy days are misty and cloudy and create beautiful panoramic views from time to time. Winter days are clear and are most enjoyable in the villages. In several ways, Himachal Pradesh is a land of beautiful scenic valleys, pastures, ravines and natural glimpses. Take the examples of Chanshal Valley's mountains of peace, Taalraa's moonlit mountains, Jubbal Kupped's beautiful pastures, the table land of Tumroo and the natural impressions of "Ishon mountain" are among the best examples of prestine scenic beauty.

Explorers Paradise: The place is quite fascinating for the botanists, environmentalists, nature lovers, trekkers and explorers from the far off places. The Gatoo forest land, Reothal Mata Temple Complex, Reothal forestland, mountain peak of Ishon and the expansion of Deiya forests is full of amazing cultural and natural heritage. The whole expansion of the forests and mountain peaks is a heaven for trekkers and explorers. Deiya Bazar has some shops and local restaurants to enjoy tea and food.

Trekkers and Adventure Lovers: The natural charm and the scenic beauty of Ishon mountain peak and Pyuntra Valley is quite indispensable. The highly beautiful and commanding views of the surrounding forests and villages from "Ishon" Mountain Peak is quite impressive and full of scenic landscapes. Here is the best example of nature matching.

Adventure Sports: The whole of Pyuntra Valley is full of beautiful pastures and apple orchards. During winter, when there is heavy snowfall, the whole of Achalti valley is full of snow and is known for its finely built natural slopes suitable for skiing, skatting and snow landscape study.

Herbal Tracks: There are 160 medicinal plants, aromatic herbs and wild flowers in the famous Pyuntra Valley. Among the medicinal herbs there are 31 precious traditional medicinal plants and herbs most suitable for medicinal values, some of them are being used for the purpose of curing fatal diseases. There are traditional doctors also who take proper care for the patients and treat them quite seriously. Sometimes, it takes two months to root out the disease. The disease is cured permanently with proper diet and herbal medicines.

The herbal tracks are organised to provide knowledge and practical experience among the students from school and colleges so that they may learn many things related to medicinal herbs and their proper utilisation in the curing of fatal diseases. It provides a lot of practical knowledge and experience to the herbal explorers. Most of the vegetables in the wild have medicinal qualities and some of them are of aromatic nature.

The herbal tracks in the past one decades have become quite popular among the explorers, trekkers, tourists and nature lovers. They pass through the Important Plant Areas (IPA) of the forests, pastures and the valleys and learn a lot of things about wild herbs. It is quite exciting to see the medicinal plants and wildflowers.

Nature Watching: To explore beautiful valley of Pyuntra is an exciting experience in life. It is an excellent place for the purpose of birds and nature watching activities. The whole Pyuntera valley, Deiya forests, Chaupal forests and other patchland forests are some of the very outstanding places for nature exploration and photographic activities.

Bird Watching: The Pyuntera Valley and Deiya forests area are an ideal place for bird watching during the summer as well as winter. During summer from March to June the area remains full of wild birds, pheasants, wild fowls, turtle dove, wild blue pigeon, skylark, Koel, Peeyu, Kaffoo hornbill, and various other clourful birds. It is quite exciting to watch them. We can watch the birds, either very close with our eyes or at a distance with the help to telescope.

The Exciting Fauna and Flora: The Pyuntra Valley and the Ishon mountains area is quite famous for the wild animals. There are beautiful colonies of wild plants, trees and bushes. Among the mammal are wild goat, (Ghoral), mountains deer, tiger, leopard, bear, fox, jackal, rabbit, ghweed, kakhad (very small deer like a calf) are found in Ishon, Deiya and Chaupal forest ranges. Among the bird fauna, Monal Pheasant, Koklash, Khaleej Pheasant, wild fowls, brown horn bill, Kingfisher, Ratnal, Palash, Jaju Rana, Teetar, Bater, Chakore, Skylark, Huppoe, Woodpecker (spotted) and forest singer are among the beautiful birds for the great enjoyment.

Among the singing birds Kaffoo, Karaoon, Baanseri, handshod, Peeli Peelang, red finch, black finch and black pisty are among the most beautiful singing birds in the wild of Pyuntra Valley.

Besides this, there are numerous reptiles, grey snakes, black snakes, cobra, diamond back, red snakes, green snakes and white spotted snakes are commonly found is the valley. The valley is a heaven for various species of colourful insects, butterflies, honey bees and fly insects etc. Among the reptiles are lizard, red, blue, grey and red, black white spotted lizards are common here.

The Flora: Pyuntra Valley is a heaven for rare wild flowers, alpine plants, trees, bushes, medicinal herbs, creepers, ornamental plants, ferns, moss and other various aromatic plants and herbs. The terrestrial orchids are among the most exciting plant species in the Ishon and Deiya forest range.

Orchids: The Ishon mountain and foot hills are known for numerous species of terrestrial orchids. Here we can locate, the most beautiful dark red and golden flowers of Lady's slippers, yellow flowering common orchid, yellow-green flowering middle heights orchids and several other small varieties of orchids are found in the moisturous land of Ishon, Reothal and other steep slopes of the mountain. The orchids are still the most exciting and beautiful plants in the world.

Ferns: The ferns are the most impressive plants in the Ishon mountain area. There are several types of ferns in the valleys, pasture lands, rock lands and amidst the dark forests of "Ishon" foothills. There are plenty of fern bushes into the fern forests of Ishon. The Dragon fern, spider's fern, the edible fern (Lingad), ornamental ferns, single blade ferns and moisture loving ferns are quite popular in the Ishon foot hills and valleys. During our exploration activities, we had located many beautiful colonies of ferns in the Ishon mountain, and its surroundings.

Moss: The moss is the most beautiful, tiny and loving plant in the wild of Ishon mountains. There are three types of moss plants in the wild of Reothal and Ishon. The first type is from semi-temperate areas with large capsul and dwart plant, second is small capsule with average moss plant, third is alpine moss with needle like capsule and needle like long plant up to three inches high. The plants are evergreen and most loving tiny plants in the world. Moss are among these tiny plants who came first in the world. The larger plants and trees came later on. In this way, moss have great importance to our life to study the plant kingdom and its evolution in the later stages.

8

Pyuntra Valley and Woodville Orchards

Pyuntra Valley is called the "Heaven of Chaupal". It is 14 Km from Nerwa and 45 Km. from Chapual. Pyuntra is also called "Everygreen Valley" due to its evergreen forests and beautifully scattered woodlands and apple orchards. The sacred mountains of Ishon (The Crown of Pyuntra Valley) Reothal Mata complex and Mahan Dhak are not only famous for their greenery and beauty but are best examples of trekking and rock climbing also. The valley itself is a nature's peaceful paradise. The Woodville Orchards, Woodville Hut and the well built helipad have opened new vistas for the development of eco-tourism. This provides employment to the local people and the promotion of tourism activities in Himachal Pradesh. The Woodville Orchards are known at national and international level for their natural charm, enchantment and beautiful panoramic views. The VIP visitors call Pyuntra the "Evergreen Valley" or "The Heaven of Chaupal" and like to see it to the closest of their hearts.

PYUNTRA

Woodville Orchards: "It is a heaven", explain a group of writers and nature lovers from foreign countries. After riding above the Pyuntra valley in Chaupal tehsil. The place is 14 kilometers from the busy town of Nerwa and makes a steep ride while trekking through valley to valley and peak to peak. The highest mountain peak is Ishon above 10,000. The people from far and near come here to offer Puja and have a great respect and regard for Mother Goddess in Ishon, the temple site. Devi Mata Reothal, Kyalu Devta have got much more importance among the domestic and religious tourists of the valley.

A modern bus route is in operation because of the efforts of Kunwar Uday Singh a businessman and statesman of Jubbal state. He is also the owner of Woodville Palace Resorts. Shimla and Woodville Orchards in Nerwa. This is the natural mountain resort in Himachal where the trekkers and tourists from far and near of the country visit in summer holidays and camp at the mountain top. Both the religious and adventure tourists come for trekking and Puja ceremony in this area. Woodville Orchards has become popular for professional businessman's holiday. It is a permanent stay point for successful planning and meetings. A large majority of them comes to spend some days with their families into the lap of nature. The Ishon, also known as the Crown of Pyuntra Valley. The Reothal and Deiya mountain forests have become popular among the small budget tourists. For the most auspicious trekking expeditions among the outdoor adventure lovers it provides a natural entertainment during winter as well as summer. The Pyuntra Valley offers a lot of flora and fauna to the lovers of wildlife, wild flowers, alpine plants and a variety of birds, bees and butterflies. There are sixty species of butterflies in the Pyuntra Valley.

The people from adventure clubs and Nature Lovers Clubs enjoy life in the wild of Pyuntara during summer holidays. Those whose life is the wrecked and jaded with the hustle and bustle of city life Woodville Orchards is nature's peaceful paradise in the wild of Pyuntra. It is a place with nature's beauty and peace. It provides relief to those who want to get peace and serenity in the wild. The people are very much conceived with the belief that Woodville Orchards can play a marvellous role in the development of tourism in the region as it offers all the beautiful things to the explorers of nature. This place is going to be the film makers paradise in the near future.

The wild flowers, alpine forests, and the bird life is rich in the valley in the summer days. The Important Plant Areas and Important Bird Areas have encouraged the nature lovers and bird watchers to come here.

Pyuntra Valley is the "Heaven of Chaupal" and most suitable tourist resort in Chaupal Tehsil. The Woodville Orchards is a jewell in the region which is envisaged in the development of the area through eco-tourism, nature conservation and people's participation in tourism and trekking activities. The surrounding nature of Woodville Orchards in Pyuntra Valley is quite impressive.

There are two beautiful villages in Pyuntera known for annal festivals with large gathering. Silodi and Paulia are surrounded with orchards and cedar forests. There are two families of Thakurs and ten families of Harijans in Paulia. All celebrate their fairs and festivals with great rejoice. Silodi is a village of Thakurs and an equal number of Harijans live here. All have common religious festivals in the area. The social harmony and co-existence is alive here.

Travelling through the Pyuntra valley is not only peaceful and enjoyable but full of thrill also. Kedi in Pyuntra is a village to enjoy life during festivals. It is a fascinating place with beautiful farmlands. The place is plain, fertile and with scattered orchards in Kedi. The Woodville Orchards have a beautiful helipad, well constructed roads. It is widely known for tourists, ideal place for film shooting locations. The Woodville Orchards is a fascinating place in the area and covers a large portion of land. A part of the region is mountaineous, rocky and uneven. When we are at Gatoo, a part of Woodville Orchards, the Valley is full of panoramic views.

The Orchards

The apple orchards in Pyuntra are full of scenic beauty when they are ripe. During apple season the whole environment is full of apple fragrance. During flowering season the whole valley is full of honeybees and butterflies. The Woodville Orchards is the largest and most popular orchard in the region which is full of apple trees and the flowering bushes. The Mahan Dhak, Reothal Wilderness, Ishon Peak and Golanu Table land are among the beautiful sites for picnic and holiday camping. The Woodville Orchards includes a beautiful cottage and a wellbuilt helipad with nice staff quarters. There are other residential arrangements for tourists and business executives coming for a short stay or holidaying in the valley. And the woodville orchards remains a heaven to all of them.

The Forests: The forestland of Pyuntra is full of amazing beauty and nature's fascination. The alpine trees and wild flowering bushes are abundantly scattered all over the mounatin slopes. The Reothal and Ishon forests are an example of wilderness management and ecotourism activities in Pyuntra Valley. During summer, we can face rich mountain bird fauna including song birds. Gatoo Khanti forests in Pyuntra are considered Asia's most dense forests.

The Wild Flowers: Ishon is the Crown of Pyuntera Valley which makes it a highest peak in the area. The most impressive glimpse of the Pyuntera Valley is visible from Gatoo (8500'). When the apple trees are in full blooms with flowers it creates a very amazing scene. The sweet fragrance of wild flowers in the air compells us to roam over valley to valley and peak to peak to enjoy the spring season. It re-energises and revitalises our spirits to recharge our body to work for a longer period. The place is a heaven for poets, writers, environmentalists, trekkers and businessmen who come here to relax into the lap of mother nature and just to refresh their mood. The Ishon mountain is full of wild flowers, terrestrial orchids, aromatic herbs and mountain top wild flowers and vegetables which regularly face the strokes of cool breeze. The sweet fragrance of the wild flowers makes a happy journey through the forest routes. The Gatoo orchards, Woodville orchards, Reothal Orchards and forestland and Ishon are a beautiful example of alpine vegetation and wild flowers. Besides eco-tourism, the religious tourism is more popular in the area as the people visit the Banad Devta temples in Silodi, Reothal Mata, Kali Mata in Ishon and Golanu Devta to offer "Puja" and other religious ceremonies. There is a beautiful temple of Goddess Kali over Mount Ishon and a Dharam Shala for tourists to stay at night. The mountain top of Ishon is a heaven in itself.

The Wild Birds: Most of the important wild birds are found here. The Monal Pheasant, Cheer Pheasant, Skylark, Koel, Red finch, Kaffoo, Hanshod, Hilansh, Brown hornbill are a good recreation. The other song birds are quite familiar in the forests to Ishon and Gatoo. The valley is a bird watcher's paradise. Pyuntra Valley is quite famous for birds like teeter, wild fowl, chakor, ghugati, kocklash and alpine bird karaoon are found here in the wild of forests. The other birds like Red - finch, Suradi, Laughing bird and other beautiful song birds are found here and sing in the wild of Reothal forest. It becomes a heaven for song birds during the spring days. The Ishon mountain, Reothal and Gatoo are surrounded by the beautiful forest and are a best exploration and trekking points for summer days.

The Nature Watch: The whole landscape of Pyuntra valley is full of greenery. During July and August. Pyuntera is called natures green paradise by the local villagers. It is a best trekking point for tourists and trekkers coming from far and near. The natural forests and grasslands are a beautiful place to relax in the lap of nature. Pyuntra is an ideal example for nature - watching as most of the part of it is visible directly at one view point. When the apple crop is ready it becomes more fascinating and enjoyable. The environment becomes full of sweet fragrance from apple fruits. The whole area is a perfect example of nature-watching as most of the terrains and beautiful mountains face us directly from the front. The nature lovers and bird watchers visit this place so often. There are two nature watch clubs in Paulia and Silodi villages to educate the people about the gifts of nature.

The Rocks: The rocks are so hard, tough and fearsome that it becomes quite difficult so climb them as they are shaped into a steep slope. Howerver, they are best examples for rock-climbing and establishing new trekking routes through the accessible slopes amidst the rocks. The rocks of Tableland Golanu, Mahan Dhak, Reothal slopes and Ishon mountains are quite fearsome but enjoyable for riding.

The climbing routes are deceitful and one should take extra care while trekking through the the Mahan Dhak, Dhaddu Rock Square, Golanu Tableland, road side rocks in the way to Kedi village, Reothal wildland and rocks at the mountain slops are among the beautiful examples of rock climbing in Pyuntra Valley. The rocks and slopes near Bijmal Village are not only impressive but easy to climb and enjoy the trekking expeditions. Bijmal is the most beautiful village to visit. In Pyuntera Valley, Silodi is the only village to enjoy life in perfect peace into the surrounding of nature. Silodi, Paulia, Tikri, Kedi and other villages are quite interesting to visit and study the social and cultural life there.

Achalti valley: The Achalti valley above the Chandrawali village is certainly a scenic place to enjoy. Nature watching, bird watching and paragliding can be enjoyed in the valleyes and pastures. It is a heaven for high profile business class as well as to common trekkers and nature lovers. The peculiarity of Achalti valley is that it is surrounded by beautiful wild lands and most fascinating pastures.

The tranquility of wide natural pastures and valleys of the Pyuntra provides a welcome change. Endless orchards of apple crops, the deep fertile vallies, small villages, with peaceful homesteads dot the pastoral landscapes. Relaxing activities in natures bird watching, hiking, horse riding and nature-watching enchance the enjoyment of a true Indian experience.

Scenic-diversity: The vallies and pastures are a natural recreation to a trekker. The place is frequented by the lovers of outdoor activities such as trekkers, mountaineers, explorers religious explorers, scholars, writers, environmentalists, businessmen and the lovers of nature. Pleasurable resorts, hospitable people and small huts amidst orchards known as "Dogri" are abound in the area. The scenic diversity is the most imporant attraction of Pyuntra Valley.

When the apple orchards are fully bloom the beauty of Pyuntra Valley is quite scientillating and full of enchantment. During the picking seasons, the fragrance of fruits fills the air and impressively make it more beautiful when we see thousands of apples on trees, various colours with different apple species. At present, twenty species of apple are grown in Himachal Pradesh.

Among the wild animals mountain tiger, Gothu (large wild cat) rabbit, monkeys, langoors, bear, rattle snakes, wild fowls Western Himalayan Pheasant, Monal, Ratnal and Cheer Pheasants are found here. The wild foxes red and brown are found abundantly on this mountain region. We have located several fox caves in the valleys of mountains.

To trek through the Pyuntra Valley is an amazing experience in itself. We can enjoy true experience of life to live with nature and enjoy night life in the camps amidst the wilderness.

The temple in Ishon mountain top is at the height of 11,500' Here, religious people arrive and stay in tents during summer festivals. There are some rooms constructed by Kunwar Uday Singh of Jubbal for the welfare of devotees coming from far and near. The place has immense religious value and it is estimated that during Puja festivals some 25000 tourists and religious people arrive here to perform the Puja Ceremony.

Kunwarani Sahiba Vidhuti Singh has also done a lot of social work in this area to develop the socio-economic status of the local people by providing them important information on agriculture, ecotourism and wilderness management. She has managed to provide water connection to Goddess Reothal temple and the Silodi villagers. Both the Kunwar and Kunwarani Sahiba are quite popular and admired among the local people for their charity and social welfare activities.

March -April and May-June are the festive occasions for tourists to visit the place with ease and relaxation. There are three 'B' s Welcoming them during the flowering of apple orchards. The three 'B' s are Butterfly, Bees, and Birds. The whole place is full of enjoyment and delightful if the camp is located in the lonely and peaceful place amidst the pasture.

The whole valley is in its full bloom and flavour while there is perfect flowering in apple trees and the area is full of sweet fragrance.

The rainy days are full of enjoyment in the mountains but the roads remain full of muds and clay. The summer days are more romantic and pleasant and the whole environment is full with the buzzing of honey bees. The rainy days in this valley should be observed with great enjoyment.

Pyuntra is 14 kilometer from Nerwa by bus and six kilometers by trekking through short route. The upper Pyuntra Valley is at 6000'-8000' altitude. The Reothal Mata temple is at 8500' and Ishon is around 11,500'. The Ishon is the highest peak after Choor Chandani in the area. The Ishon mountain peak is my favourite place to enjoy night life camp in Summer as well as winter days. It is very interesting place to observe scenic beauty of other peaks and valleys. Ishon and Deiya peaks are face to face and we can trek them in two days with more joyfully with a team of scholar friends. Choor Chandani and Tharoch-Taalraa peaks are at a distance and also face to face and can be approached in three days with joyful trekking. The four nearby peaks can be trekked in a week with excellent night life camping experience. The summer days in Ishon camp life are a heavenly experiences to all of us who spend most of their time in exploring the wilderness through day and night campaigns.

During August-September the mountain peaks and valleys are fully covered with green grass, the scenic beauty is much more appealing during these months. The winter months during snowfall are more pleasant and full of nature's romance. This is the most important time for skiing, skating and essentially ideal for snow landscape study. The whole Ishon mountain peak including Kali temple and Dharmshalla remain, covered with snowfall. The whole forest land seems to be a white snow carpet over the mountains.

Importance of Eco-Tourism: The wild life exploration and adventure tourism is the other name of eco-tourism. Our planners should do their best efforts to popularise eco-tourism and Heritage tourism in Himachal Pradesh and in other parts of the country. Kunwar Uday Singh has done a lot of good things to popularise eco-tourism in this valley. Department of Tourism has admired his marvellous qualities in the establishment of resort tourism in the country. The resort tourism is already popular among the advanced nations of Western Europe.

Attracting the more Tourists

It is quite unfortunate that mass media is not reaching to those unexplored destinations of the country where there is maximum opportunity of resort tourism and event management. Through these activities, the maximum tourism activities can be organised and covered with our most modern ways of tourism plannings and successful meetings.

There should be open competition in this regard and the well trained and highly professional people should be given an opportunity to envisage their plans. In tourism industry, the people who are funding independently are doing their best in various sectors of tourism. The business meetings, successful plannings and a broad based plan is foreseen with the immense success. The tourism sector provide ample opportunity of jobs to the people. For example, storage, marketing transportation, local industry and local peoples participation involves all those related to it. Tourism sector can adjust a large number of skilled and non-skilled manpower. There should be no bottlenecks and official interference. Tourism sector provides expanded opportunities world over. It is the only industry which touches the life of almost every section of the population in a tourist destination. Aviation, hotels, food, shops, entertainment, roads and railways, art and craft are only some of the activities which are directly affected by the flow of tourists. Currently 17.7 million people in India are employed in tourism-related industries, which is 5.6 per cent of total employment. The WTTC forecasts that if India maintains a steady rate of increase, 25 million more tourists - generated jobs could be created over the next ten years. In Kerala, savvy marketing of health tourism offering ayurveda as a stress-reliever along with its alluring beach resorts has transformed the state, now neck and -neck with Rajasthan in market leasdership. Rajasthan's heritage hotels and its palace-on-wheels luxury trains are tailored to fulfil the foreign tourist's yearing to experience exotic India and the splendour of a charmed by gone era.

Tourism performance in other states is quite pathetic. A recent survey organised by the CII (Confederation of Indian Industry) reveals that despite potholed roads, garbage heaps and pesky touts foreign tourists still vote Agra as their most favoured destination—the star attraction is the Taj Mahal itself. This despite the fact that the Taj's surrounding remain in a state of disrepair and there is little else in the town to hold tourist interest, We should really take the cue from our star performers, Kerala and Rajasthan, and try to capitalise on each tourist-potential region's USP. The Union tourism ministry should give its two-decade old tourism policy a make-over and acquire a proactive and liberal outlook emphasising the importance of private initiative. As India's second largest foreign exchange earner, notwithstanding dismal tourist arrival figures just 2.5 million against seven million each to Singapore and Malaysia and five millions to China. The tourism industry should be recognised as prime investment area which has long-term potential for employment business, trade and export. The hidden benefits to tourism go beyond economic benefits-every satisfied tourist who returns to his or her country will act as a goodwill ambassador for India. This could restore tourist confidence in India especially in the wake of several incidents of harassment of tourists in recent times. We should send goodwill message to the tourists of the world through our excellent services.

Gatoo: The Horse Neck

Gatoo is known as the horse neck in the middle and right side of Ishon mountain. The horse-back and the horse-neck is a nature's manifestation and a most enjoyable relaxation point in the wild during summer as well as winter. The Gatoo Mountain is naturally moulded in such a way that it gives us an impression of a beautiful horse' neck. It is pleasant and more romantic during spring season. The trekking and exploration journeys are most enjoyable and full of inspiration in the nature.

There are numerous wild flowers, aromatic herbs and plants blooming during spring and everybody wishes to relax into the flowering pastures of Gatoo. The life is full of peace and serenity here and provides us ample rewards of natural beauty and fresh environment amidst the Oak and Cedar forests, pastures and romantic valleys.

At the neck of Gatoo, there is most beautiful point to relax amid the Deodar forests. There is a Kunwar orchards in Gatoo where there is a small and beautiful hut for day and night stay. We can explore the steep rocks, beautiful valleys, flowering pastures, important plant areas and several other wild plant nurseries, exciting varieties of terrestrial orchids, ferns, mosses, lillys and plants with amazing beauty and medicinal values in the wild.

To visit to Gatoo, we have to catch bus from Shimla to Chaupal which is 100 kilometer. From Chaupal to Nerwa by bus is 35 kilometer and from Nerwa to Silodi village it is 15 kilometer by bus. From Silodi we can rest at Woodville Orchards or in some village as paying guests. Woodville orchards is the most impressive orchards in Shimla district.

Here we can relax for one night and can approach to Gatoo by trekking through the beautiful forest land. From Woodville orchards, we can approach to Reothal Mata Temple, which is eight kilometer by trekking. From Reothal Mata Temple Gatoo is four kilometer by trekking amidst the beautiful forests and pasture land. Between Gatoo and Reothal Mata temple complex, there are several species of forest ferns, amazing wild flowering plants, beautiful grassy pastures and deodar and Kail forest patches. The trekking through this land is not only full of enjoyment and happiness but provide us a thrilling experience also with the adventures of life which transforms our travel into a very, peaceful and contented journey. The ever-remembering journey turns into the sweet memories of life when we safely return back to our homes. The impressions of Gatoo shall always stirr into on memories. The landscapes are not only known for scenic values but remain with full of knowledge of exploration activities. Some 60 years ago, Gaatoo was quite famous for mountain deers, small tigers and bears as the famous mammals moved freely in a vast stretch of forest land. Now there are a handful of mountain deers surviving in the valleys which appear only during snowfall in the winter.

The Mountain Tigers: Bears and monkies are the main inhabitants of the dense forests of Gaatoo and Deiya forest land. These are the main exploring territories of monkies, bears and tigers. There are numerous species of rabbits, wild fowls, jackals, foxes, Shahis and the mountain deers over the steep rocks amidst the wilderness.

Gaatoo Khanti is the most densely populated forest land in the world which is known for its closely populated trees and the permanent shelter for the various species of monkies and longoors in the region. The monkies and langoors inhabit the forests in the nights and day time and increase their population in this ideal inhabitation of nature. The Gaatoo nala is the sweet spring water source in the area.

Nature's Beauty and Exploration Activities: Gaatoo, the peaceful paradise of nature is known for its scenic beauty and tip on the top view points for apple orchards, villages, valleys, golden paddy and wheat fields, the green forests and gushing clear water streams in the surrounding of nature. The mountain forests, pasture slopes and the river banks are a source of great scenic beauty.

Gaatoo to Deiya forests are the best situated places for exploration activities in the area and can be enjoyed after the trekking of ten kilometers distance and then taking rest in the camp life. These are the places of natural importance, spiritual knowledge and peaceful enjoyment of life amidst the surrounding of forests and flowering pastures. The beautiful landscape of Gaatoo can be approached by direct trekking through Nerwa, Pujarli, Silodee and then to Gaatoo, the wonder land of the Horse Neck.

During our trekking and exploration activities we face numerous species of plants, insects and butterflies during the months of summer. The mother earth here is more romantic, inspiring, exciting and full of natural charm and enjoyment. The gushing fresh water streams, dripping rocks, sparkling waterfalls and sweet fragrance of the mountain flowers and aromatic herbs fill the whole environment with scented smell.

***Orchid Hunting*:** The orchids are the most costly and most loving plants in the world. Some 300 species of them are found in the wilds of mountains. There are so many species of terrestrial orchids in the mountains, pastures forests and steep valleys. Some of them quite exciting and so loving that it becomes quite difficult for a plant lovers to detach themselves emotionally from the affection of plants. Either we have to uproot the plant for our collection or we have to leave it intact in the nature just observe and enjoy its beauty for a longer time. At that time we had to decide that if we believe the philosophy of nature conservation we will have to leave the plant in the nature and try our best to protect it so that we may see it again.

In the wild while trekking through one mountain to another mountain, we are in the process of finding more exciting species of orchids i.e. lady's slipper, alpine yellow green orchid (with large tubers), white orchid and in the semi-tropical zones in the valleys. The comb-flower orchids are quite common to observe in the mountains. Sometimes it becomes a recreation during trekking expeditions when we find an exciting orchid plant just after every ten meters distance in the mountain slopes. And it becomes more enjoyable when we get a lady's slippers plants with numerous flowers sparkling on it in the wild.

Orchid hunting is a very good hobby in the wild when we trek from mountains to mountains and valleys to valleys.

We can also hunt for some mountain lily plants with most impressive flowers and because they are wild and most exciting in form and beauty.

The ferns are also for great recreation for human mind. Whenever we face some, fern bushes and fern plants, we try to classify them according to their structure, nature of growth and the quality of plants. In this way, we have classified ten types of most beautiful ferns found between the heights 6000' upto 13000'. We have seen the small plants to Dragon ferns and Spiders ferns in the foothills, valleys and in the middle of the mountains inside the dense forests. This was a kind of great excitement which we had experienced during our trekking and exploration expeditions in the mountains upto 8,000′ height. Our last attempt was upto the snowline of Chaukhambha Mountain which is upto 24000'. Chaukhambha is a beautiful mountain with a vast playground of snow within its four mountain pillars. We are in the preparations of our next expeditions to Chaukhambha.

Fern Hunting: In the pasture slopes, forests, valleys and river banks, the fern hunting is an ideal hobby and a best pass time for the explorers and trekkers who want to enjoy natural beauty and various forms of plants like fern and orchids. There are some small species of ferns in the Himalayn regions. The ferns came into existence some 360 million years ago. They are older than land animals. These fern forests were thriving on earth upto 200 million years. The other plants to search out are mountain lilies, Purvat leontopodium alpinum (Himalayensis), moss, riccia, marcantia, horse tails and insectivorous plants. There are some 450 species of insectivorous plants over this earth. Among them are Nepenthes (Pitcher plant), Drosera (sundew) Dionaea (Venus fly trap) Utricularia (Bladderwort or leaf bladder plants) and Sarracenia are quite amazing insectivorous plants found in the nature. We should find out them in the nature and observe their physical forms, their mechanism of trapping the small insects and their technic of catch, trap and digest them. It is very-very interesting hobby as well as a passtime game among the students on outdoor education trip to vast forest land. We can learn ourselves first to educate other people later on. Such activities can be encouraged in every schools and colleges to protect the nature like orchid and fern hunting we can locate Bhojpatra (Birch tree) in the upper heights of Chanshal (Himachal) and Badrinath (Uttranchal) and can make them the best exploration activities in the mountains. Their protection and conservation should be as certained in these activities.

Years ago, after this the flowering ferns evolved on the earth. At present there are 20,000 species of ferns growing all over the world excluding deserts and snow lands. The fern species are classified in the phylum pteridophyte. It is also known as filicophyta. The group also referred as polypodiophyta or polypodiopsida. The vascular plants come under tracheophyte. The study of fern is called Pteridology. The person who studies ferms it is known as Pteridologist. There is different terminology to seedless plants and advance seed plants.

There are amazing fern forests in Queensland, Australia, Southern, New South Wales and Tasmania. Dicksonia Antarctica is a soft tree fern found in queens land to Tasmania. It is 15 meter tall tree. Cyathea cunninghumii is a slender tree fern which is 20 meter tall. There are several other species of fern in the southern new South Wales and Tasmania where these have become a great source of botanical tourism to the Australian government.

In the same vein, orchids (orchidacaeae family) are the largest and most diverse flowering plants (Angiosperms) families with over 800 described genera and 25,000 recognised species. Some sources given 40,000 species. There are another 100,000+hybrids produced by horticulturists. About 800 new species are added each year. These are commercial plants and are sold by flower exporters.

Orchids like Tulips are the best selling orchids in the flower markets of different countries. Vanilla planifolia and two other Vanilla species are highly of commercial value.

Madagaskar is the leading producer of Vanilla seed powder in the world. In 2005, it produced 73 lakh metric tons of Vanilla powder used in the flavour of Coca-Cola company. Vanilla is a very labour intensive crop since the flowers have to be pollinated by hand. It is considered as one of the most profitable crop for small family farms.

The City of Orchids. The city of orchids has become a great source of tourism in Moyobamba, a city capital of San Martin Region in Northern Peru. There are 50,000 inhabitants in the city and some 3,500 species of orchids are native to the area. That's why Moyobambais called the City of Orchids in the world.

In the Himalayan states of India, the ferns and orchids areas have become popular with name of fern trails and orchid trails among the tourists from far and near.

9

The Moonlit Mountains of "Taalraa"

Tharoch is some 35 km from Nerwa and Nerwa is 135 km from Shimla via Chaupal. Taalraa wilderness in Tharoch is also known as "the moonlit mountains", as in day and night it gives an impression of moonlit nights. Taalraa is the most famous wild life sanctuary at 18 km. from Tharoch town. Earlier, in the British Raj Tharoch was a Princely State and had all the facilities of hospital, court, range office and other systems of a lively state. The King here was known for his honesty, intelligence, moral values and efficient administration which the people remember till to date. Taalraa is a most beautiful wilderness known for its enchantment and peaceful environment. All the Western Himalayan birds and pheasant are found here. The wood felling is totally banned in Himachal. It has turned into a more dense and lively forest for exploration activities. Taalraa in many ways, is a heaven on earth.

Tharoch: If the Taalraa peak is a called the crown of these roof for Gurhaad Village and saves it from storms and other natural calamities. Gurhaad, a small village is trekkers paradise and is situated on a table land rock. The surrounding more beautiful and lively. Tharoch is a heaven for most of the residents of the area. Peace and contentment is prime source of inspiration in life. The feeling of contentment exists in this erstwhile Princely State and most of the modern families have traditional way of living. Rana Baljit Singh former Raja of Tharoch is a scholar, writer and well wisher of the people. He did his best to provide jobs and education to the local youths. The people worship Lord Mahasu day and night. Rana Baljit Singh, a saintly person with great human qualities, is doing his best efforts for the upliftment and development of Tharoch through guidance and good will mission. The Palace and temple of Mahasu in Tharoch is in shambles because of negligence and without proper maintenance. The Ranas have not proper funds to maintain this historical building imbibed with the cultural heritage of Tharoch. This gives us a lot of pain that pillars of our cultural heritage is in shambles. The villages like Kutangan, Gurhad and other small hamlets are a scene of enjoyment and excitement to the newcomers and explorers in the area. The people are most hospitable and the women are polite and generous. "Jaagraa" is a colourful festival and celebrated in the month of August. It is the most auspicious festival in the area. The people of Tharoch are most peace loving over this part of earth. Pather Chauth, Saaji and Jaagra are the most famous festivals of the area and rejoiced with great performanced by a and all.

Tharoch and Chaur Basha : The height of Tharoch is 7500' and the Taalra of peak is about 11,000'. It is among the most impressive tourist places of Himachal Pradesh. It is known among the explorers and trekkers and the complovers. Chaur Basha is about 8000' and is a magnificent place above Tharoch. It is in a shape of table "land". Chaur - Basha is a place of peace, serenity and natural enchantment. It is the most enjoyable and peaceful place on earth. It is situated amidst the cedar and oak forests. It has a natural helipad and impressive apple orchards.

Sainj is a small and beautiful village dotted with green valley of Mashranh. It has a very small a population. It is 25 km from Nerwa and seven km. from Tharoch. This is a beautiful village with vegetable gardens. The population of Tharoch is 3000. Tharoch is the most religions village as their great Lord Mahasu lives here in the temple inside the palace. All the people of the area are emotionally attached with this Temple. Tharoch is also called the village of ceremonies and festivals. Religious ceremonies are organised every month. Every year, there are religious and ritual activities among the village people.

Sometime, the girls, boys and old people also come under the influence of Goddess Kali, Lord Narsimha, Lord Mahasu and Maheshwar Devta. Such scenes of Gods and Goddesses dancing together are quite spectacular in the local ceremonies of religious festivals or worship of God in Tharoch. The people have great faith in Lord Mahasu and abide with their socio-religious traditions and cultural heritage.

Tharoch: The Princely Village

Tharoch is surrounded by small pastures and forest land and is also called the nature's village. There are beautiful grass lands and finest cedar trees and Kail forests, grassy pastures, valleys and rocks. We can face beautiful mountain peaks of Taalraa, Moraloo, Kangar an Sheela from the palace of Tharoch. Chaur basha is one Km from Tharoch and is a beautiful picnic spot. We can view all the local mountain peaks. From there, most spectacularly, is the view of Taalraa mountains. It is most conspicuous and enchanting pasture in many ways.

Tharoch is surrounded by small hamlets and villages and towards North side there is a huge and most enchanting pasture of Moraloo, surrounded by pine, oak and cedar forests. The other peaks are Taalraa, Kangar and Sheela village roof top. The above peaks are a magnificent examples of pastoral management and ecotourism. Taalraa is famous for its wildlife sanctuary and there are 100 birds in this high attitude forest. During snow fall Taalraa produces most amazing views of snowland. As if a white carpet is spread over Talra mountains. This is the real occasion for snow sports and the adventure lovers.

The Tharoch Palace with Lord Mahasu temple is an exceptional asset to visit. It is among the most ancient palaces in Himachal Pradesh, mainly constructed with wood and stones. It is a marvellous example of the ancient architecture and cultural heritage. The fairs and festivals and religious activities here are a subject of anthropological studies. The people worship various local Gods and Goddesses and have abound faith in them.

Among them the main temples in Tharoch includes: Narsimha Devta, Kali Mata, Durga Mata, Thakur Dwara, Shirgul Devta, Sri Ram Temple and Maheshwar Devta Temples are located here with great divine values and human importance.

Tharoch is surrounded by magnificent mountain peaks. Among the important one are Chaurbasha, Moraloo, Taalraa,

Kangar and Sheela mountains which make a very outstanding combination of a mountain range and pasture lands almost accessible for trekking and skiing in winter months during snowfall.

During spring time, the whole landscape fills up with greenery and wild flowers. Tharoch is a heaven for tourists, trekkers, explorers and nature lovers. The famous wildlife sanctuary, Taalraa is quite popular among travellers and outdoor lovers. Taalraa in itself is a heaven for nature explorers, bird watchers and trekkers. It is an ideal place for night life camping and other exploring activities.

Taalraa is 18 km. from Tharoch and the distance can be covered both ways in a single day if we proceed on early at 4A.M. in the morning. For our social study we can visit the villages like Kutangan, Chaur-Basha and Gurhaad. From Tharoch, Chaur-Basha and Kutangan are at one and half kilometer distance. Gurhad is at eight kilometer distance. From Gurhad, we can proceed on to Taalraa with great expectations enriching our experiences in nature watching and bird watching. Taalraa Forest Range is famous for alpine fauna and flora. During spring, the trekking routes and pastures are full of exciting wild flowers and alpine plants. This makes the whole environment more pleasant and enchanting. The valleys are full of sweet fragrance.

The Moraloo and the Moonlit Nights

"Come to Moraloo and be blessed with the grace of Lord Moraloo, the Great God of happiness and prosperity" is saying in Bairog village. The Moraloo God and Moraloo Mahadev are two Great Gods of Bairog village in the lap of Taalraa Wilderness. Bairog village is situated amidst the trees of oak and deodar which gradually expands into a vast stretch of forests. It is the nature's peaceful paradise and makes an interesting account of its natural beauty, scattered orchards, pastures and agricultural fields. Moraloo mountain is the crown of Bairog village and the surrounding pastures are nature's peaceful playgrounds.

The Moraloo pasture is surrounded by cedar, oak and pine forests. It is expanded upto 3-4 kilometers. At a corner of Moraloo Pasture is the temple of Lord Moraloo, the God of milk and Ghee. Also known as the Great God of wealth and happiness and brings prosperity to those who worship and adore him.

Location: From Delhi we can reach to Shimla by bus or by jeep. From Shimla, we can proceed on to Chaupal which is 100 kilometers by bus. From here we can ride a bus to Nerwa, a distance of 35 kilometers. From Nerwa, we can get a bus in the evening for Tharoch also 35 kilometers. From Tharoch we can trek to Bairog village which is 3 kilometers with a beautiful serpentive trekking route admidst the forest. From Bairog village we can move upto Moraloo Devta Pasture which is also 3 kilometers from the village. Here are the beautiful wide pastures of Moraloo. Just near the corners of Moraloo Pastures there are two beautifully manifested rock hillocks also known as Moraloo Mahadev and Moraloo Parvati. The duo husband wife are in equal shape and size standing side by side. The people gaze them with religious affinity and worship them as Mahadev and Parvati. The mountains are known with the name of "Moraloo Mahadev".

The people have great respect for these two rock hillocks and worship them when they are with their cattles in the forests. The "Moraloo Mahadev" and "Moraloo Parvati" are visible from the side of Kutangan village. Though, the beautiful village of Kutangan have no any temple in the village, nor there is any symbolic temple rocks. But the Moraloo Mahadev and Parvati are a great attraction to all of them in the outskirts of the Moraloo Pastures. The hillocks are natures most impressive manifestation.

Moraloo and Moonlit Nights: The plain pastures of Moraloo are a great source of recreation and enjoyment to all of us who have settled for camplife. During the full moon nights the rocks are shining, the pasture land is beautifully covered with light and the trees are in peace and meditation. The cool breeze passes through our faces and puffs our hairs towards back–a good respite in the moonlit nights. There is silence when we are engrossed in talking about our plans and future activities in the wild in the coming days. The wild fowls and birds chirp and wild animals make some hissing noise in the nearby forests. This all provides us immense delight and we think that we are not alone in the moonlit night in this wildland. During spring days, the moonlit nights provide us a lot of time for speculation, to think about future plans, writing diaries photography, trekking, exploration and camping in the wild. These plans are made by mutual co-operation in the group meetings and are initiated in the next campaign. The moonlit nights were most enjoyable during our campaign by trekking amidst the forests. The moonlit nights" were full of inspiration and beautiful for us. We spent some days in Tharoch, Bairog, Moraloo and Taalraa wilderness. We got a unique experience in the wild during moonlit nights. (1) The closeness of nature and man was first observed by all of us in the moonlit nights (2) It was dead silence in the moonlit nights. Upto 8 O'clock in the night, it was very sweet chirping of song birds but after that it became dead silence. In the evening, all the wild birds start chirping with sweet songs and make a beautiful noise which remain, upto eight O'clock. The noise of the night insects also makes us pleased in the moonlit nights. It becames more and more enjoyable to walk through the Moraloo pastures and forests in the moonlit nights. It is a heavenly experience to spend nights in Moraloo.

The Moonlit Nights: A Heavenly Experience Amidst Dense Forests: The Moraloo forest is a kind of fairyland. The patches of Deodar, Kail, Oaks and other local plants and bushes welcome us in the silence of the wild. The morning and evenings are full of sweet songs of wildbirds and that is one of the best recreation for the bird lovers. When there is full moon and the nights are warm, the life in Moraloo can be compared with the heaven. The warmth of the grass and the closeness of nature provides us with a sense of the celestial beauty of nature and the knowledge of God. Here, to become close to God means we have to remain near the nature. In true sense, nature is also a form of Godly creation. There are several species of wild animals, birds, butterflies, insects, honey bees and the reptiles, trees and plants which get shelter into the lap of mother nature. And every animal and plant plays its role well in the nature. Some birds chirp, insects make whistles and the fire beatle shine here and there by flying in the air. When we take tea or coffee or have food in the wild it provides us immense pleasure to watch them. It provides us knowledge and enjoyment in the closet of nature. In the winter camps, the tea and coffee provides us peace, happiness and satisfaction as we relax in the lap of nature. When we are too much tired because of our continuous trekking, tea break or coffee break provides solace to our body and mind. This is the thing when we acquire full enjoyment of life during the moonlit nights. We can relax inside our costly sleeping bags in the open of the sky or inside our tents. If somebody wants to enjoy life his or her fullest, Moraloo is the wonderland. It has to offer a lot of things to the tourists and trekkers who love to explore the mountains.

The Romantic Forest Land: There are so many beautiful forests, natural sites and wonderland over this earth. Moraloo is one of them. It has beautiful pastures, Cedar forests, Oak patches, Kail patches and local mountain trees and bushes. The peculiarity of this forest is that there are forests within a vast forest. All the forests lands are densely populated and the open lands between the forests are plain treeless and beautifully located. This is widely used by the nature watchers, explorers and camp lovers. These are unspoilt prime forests and are amazingly straight and densely populated.

In the morning when the sunrays pour over the landscape of Moraloo, it shines with golden brightness as the whole landscape shines with lush green carpet of the vegetable.

The natural valleys, ravines, slopes, rocks, woodlands and patch lands are architected into a very marvellous way. Some wildlands and rock shelter are manifested in such a way as if it was constructed to create a multipurpose tourists avenue on this earth.

There are beautiful gushing water streams below the heights of Moraloo which flow through the wildlands of Bairog and Kutangan. These sweet water springs are the results of cedar and oak forests in Moraloo. It is said that some 100 years back, the whole area was fully covered by the cedar and oak forests. Later on, the increasing human pressure has reduced the oak forests as it was being used for fuel in the villages. It was also used in burning in the forest by the Gujjars and Gaddis during night stay. The whole night remained full of stone-fire. The Bakkerwals and Bhediwals were always using this fire in the forests whether it was day or night, particularly during the winter nights.

The peaks, plains and the slopes at Moraloo create a most impressive scenic view. The forests are enchanting and romantic during morning sunrise.

The Water Springs: The water springs near Moraloo create a beautiful glimpses. They are the most enjoyable gifts of the nature to man as they emerges up from the lower heights of the mountains and have medicinal qualities. The mineral water generates from the rock cavities and is sweet and digestive in nature. When we approach to Moraloo we do not forget to collect this water for our use. This water increases hunger, makes us feel well, the brain functions very efficiently, it means the water is completely pollutionless and bacterialess. It helps in improving health, digest food properly and increases human activities both at home and out door.

The Camplife in Chaur Basha Forests : If we see it from the point of view of recreation, it becomes more enjoyable at night. We spend some days in perfect peace and serenity. This also encourages our creative field of writing poems, essays and travel diary. Seeing the importance of the wide pastures, it can be organised at the corner of the wild land or at the "Gumtee" in the pasture which is surrounded by three sides and remains warm in the winter as well as summer. This "Gumtee" is knwon as warm place. It is a wide cave like structure where no external airs or harsh storm penetrates inside the tents. The forests above the Tharoch and Chaur Basha are full of pristine beauty and most enjoyable for campsites.

Mokina-Aurhal-Waterfall: When we move downwards to a gushing water stream in the valley of Bharmana village, we face a beautiful sparkling water fall. This is the most enchanting water fall in the area and provides an impressive view from the opposite side of the waterfall. The place is useful for hydro-electric projects. It can be used for film shooting and the films based on wild life and natural sites. From Bharmana to Mokina-Aurhal waterfall, Sheela Panchayat to Sheela-Kangar mountain, it can be an ideal trekking and exploration activity. We can spend one day at the Kangar top as camplife experience and come back the next day. There are five more mountain peaks near the area to explore. It becomes quite pleasant to move from one village to another village and live with the experiences of life. But the forest life is more pleasant than the villages. This is my personal experience in life while moving and trekking from mountain to mountain and forest to forest. It is adventurous as well as full of enjoyment.

The Caves: While trekking from place to place in the area, we came across to various big and small rock-caves which are quite safe and enjoyable during the night time. We have seen such caves in Gurhaad Valley enroute to Taalraa Wilderness. Near the Bharmana-Mokina-waterfall, there is a beautiful ancient cave and 5-6 people can be adjusted there. There are some beautiful caves near the Golanoo rock and enroute to Bijmal from Woodville Orchards. The caves can be used during the harshest climates also.

The Campfire: Whether it is summer or winter the campfire always protects us and provides us heat and energy. This heat energy protects us from the colder environment inside or outside the camp. The campfire can always be enjoyed amidst the forest. The camp members may surround the fire and enjoy their winter days. At the height of 14000′, there is always cold in the summer days.

Relaxing over the Pasture: When there is bright sun and we are tired by trekking, there is a great need to relax into an open pasture like Moraloo. The pastures are created into such a marvellous way that during bright sun even the cold winds do not disturb the trekkers and they take full sleep over the warm grass for some hours. The grass is quite soft, warm and dear to our body. It provides us an unique experience to relax on the warm grass in the lap of mother nature. In many ways, like human beings, the Moraloo pastures provide shelter to several beautiful wild flowers, trees, plants, aromatic herbs, medicinal herbs and green grasses. Besides this, it is a heaven for the fire beetles, insects, bees, lizards, snakes, mammals like tigers, bears, monkies, langoors, foxes, jackals, rabbits, deers and several other animals useful to man and nature. Among the bird fauna, there are a lot of song birds, kingfisher, hornbill, monal, ratnal, palash, chakor, teetar, bater and the famous skylark.

Chanshal : The mountains of Peace : We can Visit the Place by bus or taxi

From Shimla, we can proceed on to Jubbal, some 110 km. We can cover Hatkoti at a distance of 20 kilometer and Rohru at an eleven km. distance. From Rohru we can proceed on to Chirgaon some 18 km. distance. (From Rohru to Chirgaon, we have a short trekking route also). From Chirgaon we can proceed on to Tikri a beautiful village in the Valley of Pabbar river. This travelling is covered by bus or jeep upto Tikri Village. From here, we can proceed on to Larot : the 18 kilometer steep trekking distance from Tikri. This village is the gateway to Chanshal Valley. From here, some 20 kilometer upwards is the beautiful pasture of Chanshal. All the peaks in the area are upto 10,000 to 18,000' in height and can be covered by arduous trekking. Chanshal is a paradise for trekking and exploration activities.

Larot is our multipurpose base camp. From here, we can have access to various places of trekking importance. During a short stay in a base camp, we can have one or two days for trekking expeditions and come back at the to base camp Larot upto evening. To larger distance places, we can have night camp there taking readymade food with us from the base camp.

For most of the trekkers base camp is a place for multipurpose activities. From here we can approach to.

1. Maraal Daandaa, The mountain of sweet fragrance.
2. Chanshal Pasture and wildrness for exploration activities.
3. Ghasnot Pasture for night time camping.
4. Tangankha Pastures for trekking and camping.
5. Jangla Ansar Valley for shortime stay in camps.
6. Dodraa - Quaar Villages for nature exploration and cultural heritage expeditions.

The villages and temples are an example of ancient cutural values and heritage in this part of earth. The village people in the Chanshal Valleys have great religious values and spirtitual sentiments. They have several Gods and Goddesses to worship and so are the fairs and festivals. With ancient cultural values from Larot village, we can proceed on to every directions for our trekking expeditions. We can cover one place in a day or two if necessary. We can slow our speed if we want to enjoy the camplife in the pastures and explore the vast wildlands. The Chanshal Valley is the most enjoyable place for trekking, skiing, skating, hang gliding, paragliding, botanical tracks and herbal tours for the lovers of botanical wealth. To see the herbal medicines the tourists want to explore the larger parts of Chanshal pasture.

The nature watching and bird watching camps can be organised in the pasture during summer days. From top of the peak we have very fascinating views of the valleys. The wild flowers and alpine plants produce a very enchanting view from a distance. During March - April to August-September we can enjoy flowering season on the valley with our full enjoyment. The Birch Tree (Bhojpatra) is found in Chanshal. A large number of species of terrestrial orchids is found here. We have located yellow flower orchid and lady's slipper orchid here. It was most exciting to observe the beauty of orchids in chanshal valley.

"The nature beauty of chanshal valley is the most amazing in Himachal. It has become a popular destination for adventure sports. The people come here and remain in the camp from 10-20 days and go back happily." Explain Dr. Om Prakash Khagta, a doctor of domestic animals of Himachal Goverment.

"Both low budget and high budget tourists can easily be adjusted here according to their pockets." States Rana Surjan Singh, a trekker and orchardist of Tikri Village.

10

The Pastures of Sweet Fragrance

The Whole Chanshal Valley remains full of wild flowers and its surrounding pastures shine with enchanting greenery. It becomes more pleasant when the wild flowers and aromatic plants are in full bloom and the whole environment is filled with sweet fragrance. The Maraal Daandaa has this peculiar characteristics. In Pahari dialect Maraal means - fragrance or the mountain of fragrance.

The Maraal Daandaa is called the Mountains of Sweet Fragrance by the Gaddis and Gujjars of the area. It is very outstanding picnic spot, ideal for day and night life camping, exploration and trekking activities in the area. Maraal Daandaa is basically known for its scented plants and wild flowers scattered over the whole pasture. Several plants are known for their immense medicinal values.

Maraal Daandaa: As its name depicts it, Maraal Daandaa is the mountain of sweet fragrance which lingers for a longer time into the minds of people who come to trek here from far and near. It is a heaven for nature lovers and bird watchers. There are impressive mountain pasture in the Tikri region and adjoining slopes of Chanshal. The Gujjars and Gaddis enjoy life amidst nature with their herds upto the height of 18,000" feet. "Come to Maraal if you want to enjoy peace into the lap of mother nature". Explains a local Gaddi. In true sense, Maraal is a nature's peaceful paradise. The trekkers and explorers visit here to enjoy adventure sports during winter days. It has some beautiful forest patches, steep rocks and amalgamated pasture land. The trekkers enjoy its cool breeze during summer. When the spring arrives and the wild flowers and alpine herbs are in full bloom, the natural beauty of Maraal is much more impressive. The flowering season starts in March-April and July-August every year. When the pastures are in full bloom the mountains are full of sweet fragrance it becomes more pleasant here. The whole pasture is filled with scented air in the environment. Maraal Daandaa is a heaven for day and night life camping during May-June and September-October. For excellent camplife experiences, summer days are more romantic and pleasant for adventure lovers.

All the famous alpine flowers of the Western Himalayas are found in Maraal Alpine Zone. The flowers start to blossom from March - April and August - October. The trekkers, visitors and nature lovers enjoy life after a short stay in the wild of Maraal Daandaa. The green grass, herbal plants, wild flowers and moisture loving plants always welcome us into more impressive way where one can find peace and serenity. One who once visit, Maraal would not like to return back from these heavenly pastures, valleys and ravines. This has given us a very matured experience with varieties of trekking experience. It becomes more wise and lively when we explore Maraal alpine pasture through scholarly friends (environmentalists, botanists and ecologists). Maraal Daandaa is popular among those who love its ecology and rich floral diversity.

The slopes of Maraal are called the valley of sweet fragrance. We are amazed to see striking beauty of wild flowers and aromatic plants scattered into the pasture. It comes into the zone of Important Plant Area and a bird watchers paradise. Mountain crow known idiot crow or dom kauwa is found in Maraal and Chanshal. The famous birds like Monal, Ratnal, Jo jo Rana, Mountain buzzard, cry bird Kanur is found in Maraal, Tanganakha and Chanshal Valley.

Maraal Daandaa is quite popular destination among the local trekkers and grazers. It is one of the most fascinated places of the Western Himalayas which remain full of peace and serenity.

Larot: Larot is a lonely village in the wild of Chanshal and almost welcoming all sorts of explorers and trekkers to Chanshal. Larot is the gateway to Chanshal valley from where we can approach to upwards direction, straight climbing to

Chanshal peak (estimated upto 18,000'). Chandra Nahan lake is at the height of 18000' and the highest peak of Chanshal is also the same. The real Himalayas exists above the Chandra Nahan lake.

Some days can be enjoyed in Larot. It is a village surrounded by natural beauty. We can camp into the lap of nature. All the possible trekking routes to various mountain peaks lead from Larot. From Larot we can approch to Dodraa - Quaar, some 42 kilometers from Chanshal valley base camp.

Larot is a village of multipurpose stay point. It is nature's peaceful paradise where the tourists, trekkers and climbers come every year to relax into the lap of nature. We can get food, tea refreshments and night shelter at Larot. We can spend some enjoyable nights at Larot. A large numbers of social scientists come here to study the traditional values of local village communities and their fairs and festivals.

Honey Moon Valley: Larot has become a popular stay point among the newly married couples and young lovers. The main reason of this is the scenic beauty of the place and peace and serenity in the wild. For this season, we call Larot a Honeymoon Valley as most of the learned couples of the country visit this lonely place in summer and winter holidays. This has set a marvellous example in the tourists and trekkers arrivals in the valley. There is a popular saying among the local people with perfect enjoyment and rejoice. "Come Larot and enjoy a lot. Relax into the lap of beautiful pasture land and explore a new world of your own."

Larot is linked with a road from Tikri and Dhamwari. It is a passion for those who arrive here with their personal vehicles, car, mini buses, taxi cabs and tourist buses. The tours and travel agencies are doing their best in the development of domestic tourism.

Larot is linked with trekking routes from four sides. It is an amazing village developing into the wild of pastrureland. It is the most popular base camp for trekkers and explorers in Chanshal region. The Gaddis, Gujjars, trekkers, social scientists, botanists and researchers visit this place from time to time. During sunny days, the place is a real paradise on earth. It is an ideal place for camping, long time staying and research findings. It is an important location for adventure sports. A large number of plant lovers from foreign countries come here for the exploration of wild flowers and alpine plants. Chanshal is internationally known for the largest numbers of flowering plants in the Western Himalayas. The region is an ideal place for Important Plant Areas and ecological values of alpine flora. Larot is developing with the pace of time. It has become a trekkers' paradise because of its natural surrounding, ancient stone houses and cultural heritage. This is the main base camp and a permanent staying point for adventure lovers in western Himalayas of Chanshal valley. We can stay in PWD resthouse, and the rooms are available in the village also at the local rates. To study socio-religious life and the cultural heritage we can visit to Tikri, Chirgaon, Dodraa Quaar and various other villages of Chanshal valley situated at an average distance. All the villages are a great source of socio-ethnical studies and village folk life.

In this way, Larot the gateway to Chanshal Valley and Dodraa - Quaar are a great source of heritage tourism. The scenic beauty of the valleys and mountains is quite impressive.

Secondly, the surrounding nature and forests of Larot is a good source for the study of wild plants in different seasons. There exists an amazing world of herbs, plants and trees in the plant kingdom of Chanshal Valley. Larot is also a heaven of orchids, ferns, alpine moss and Lady's slipper orchids.

The wild flowers, alpine plants and trees have made it most important place to explore a world of botanical wealth. Among the mammals mountain tiger (small one), brown bear, blackbear, red bear, foxes, Gothu (a large wild cat-bird hunter), Langoors and monkeys found here. The rabbit, shahi, white-brown fox and small deer is found here.

Among the bird Fauna, there is a great numbers of birds which exists in the western Himalayan climate. The birds are Monal Pheasant (Lophorus Impejanus), cheer Pheasant, Wester Himalayan Tragopan, Jojo Rana, Ratnal, Khaleej, Koklash, brown-red spotted wood packer, large black crow and wild fowls are found in the valleys.

11

Chanshal : The Mountains of Peace

The vast pastures of Chanshal valley are spread from 18000 with 100 square km or more. The mountain slopes are full of greenery and silence hence are called the mountains of peace.

Chanshal's highest peak in the valley is known for its amazing silence and beauty. Trekkers find it pleasant enchanting and peaceful while camping at the plain pastures of Chanshal during summer as well as winter. This is the only pasture in Himachal which is most popular mountain among the foreign visitors who come here to study the unique eco-systems of this amazing land. This is an important place for the study of aromatic plants and alpine vegetation. The pasture of Chanshal valley is an amazing world in itself. The most important thing about it is that it has a different Important Plant Area zone in Western Himalayas known for bright wild flowers, herbs and moisture loving plants.

Chanshal Valley: "When you are puzzled with the hustle and bustle of city life, Chanshal will provide you solace in the lap of nature. Here, mother nature welcomes you with great care and affection", explains Major Vijay Singh Mankotia, former Tourism Minister, Himachal. Here, a proverb among the village folks and Gaddis of Western Himalayas is quite popular. "You go to any part of the world, but Chanshal will call you back whenever it requires your services. It will caress and nourish you." This is a belief among the local Gaddis and Gujjars.

We felt the sweet fragrance of flowers and herbs when we approached towards Chanshal valley. After a long arduous trekking we faced several species of flowers and fruits that were scattered in the wild of Chanshal.

On exploring the valleys and open pastures we faced several rare plants, herbs and trees while riding up to pasture after the pastures. The wild flowering plants, honey bees and sweet fragrance of aromatic plants still refreshes our mind while travelling through valley to valley. There are so many valleys in the chanshal.

Chanshal is the largest pasture, longest valley and most fascinating place for outdoor activities for trekkers, travellers and nature lovers of the world. For most of the Himachalis, Chanshal is the centre point and abode of all the trekkers and mountain lovers in this hill region. During snow fall in winter the pastures and slopes are fully covered with a fat layer of snow. Chanshal is the best examples of snow landscape study. The rare plants and trees of are found in this part of region and most of the trees and plants are on the verge of extinction. The main reason of this is:

1. The grazers and Gujjars damange a large part of botanical wealth deliberately or ignorantly. They should be taught about nature conservation activities.
2. A large part of wild plants and medicinal herbs is smuggled out by the herb smugglers and contractors who are not educated or learned at all. Due to this reason, most of the alpine herbs are on the verge of extinction.
3. To make it more workable, the grazing zones should be marked properly for Gujjars and their cattles so that specific zones of Important Plant Areas may be saved.
4. We should create safe environment zones through nature conservation activities in which the Gaddis and Gujjars also be involved.
5. Continuous felling of Birch (Bhojpatra) and other endangered alpine plants and trees have caused a great concern among the lovers of alpine ecology.

The birch tree is being wiped out from this part of land and several other plant species are on the verge of extinction. Some important botanicals have disappeared because of the continuous grazing and felling of trees by the Gujjars in the area. This has done immense damage to the forests and pastures by the grazers. Several environmental organisations in India and abroad have raised their voice against the destruction of alpine vegetation. The NGOs like Global Village of India and International Institute of Mountain Studies and Research are raising their voice against the damage of the pastures and valleys and mismanagement of the forestland in the region.

The important features of outdoor studies in Chanshal are:

1. Chanshal is the only lonely place in the region where travellers and trekkers can enjoy life with perfect peace and harmony. This inculcates a great emotional attachment with nature.
2. The mountain birds are found in large numbers in the area and most of them are spotted by the trekkers regularly. Some of the precious birds and wild animals are killed regularly by the hunters or Gujjars. The most amazing birds with different colours are found in Chanshal among the most important of them are: Monal Pheasant, Western Himalayas Tragopan, mountain owl, mountain fowls, skylark, huppoe, woodpecker, red and black finches are found here. There are also some song birds in the area. Among the mammals, mountain tiger, brown and red bears, ghoral rabbit, white brown fox, shahi, wild cat (Gothoo) are found in the temperate valleys of Chanshal.

The alpine oak, birch, (Bhojpatra), mountain sunflower, cone flower terrestrial orchids and various other alpine flowers and trees are found here with their peculiar charm and strangeness in the wild.

THE AMAZING PASTURELAND OF CHANSHAL VALLEY

Ghasnot is the name of Chanshal's world famous grassland in the interior of Chirgaon Tehsil. The whole pasture is covered with lush green alpine carpet grass and is suitable for day and night camping for summer as well as winter. An avid trekker should enjoy the taste of trekking in Chanshal in every season. This provides more confidence and prepares us to face more dreadful challenges of life. Ghasnot is a part of Chanshal pastures and makes an interesting study on its environment.

Ghasnot Pastures: Sweet fragrance from the aromatic grass and wild flowers welcomes us while passing through the

Ghasnot. It is a beautiful grassland and pasture known among the Gaddis, Gujjars and trekkers in the viscinity of Chanshal valley. These pastures are used only for grazing cattles by Gujjars.

Ghasnot is known for its nutritious grasses which helps to increase milk in the cows, buffalows and goats. The meaning of Ghasnot is "the land of grass". There are several varieties of wild grasses in this pasture which are very useful for the cattles. The Gaddids and Gujjars live here with their cattles for a longer period and after grazing the whole pasture they return back to the lowlands. This routine is completed every year with the instructions and meeting of Gujjar chiefs. The decision is made after reviewing the problems of all Gujjars. In this process. The Gujjars wander from place to place with their cattles.

The scenic beauty and slopes of Ghasnot make an strange but impressive glimplses of the nature's beautiful landscape.

The people come and go but the local people remember it as peaceful location for night stay, Camp life and gliding in the valleys during summer days. The wild land of Ghasnot has become a permanent abode with the movement of their camp life.

"Gujjar is not a Gujjar if he does not face the hardships in the wild. He has to face bitter cold in the winter and devastating torrents of rain during rainy season. In the night he has to face the attacks from tiger and bear. He has to remain in the wild to lead a rough and tough life. The government has done some good efforts to rehabilitate them in Pathri near Haridwar more than 1000 faimlies have been settled down there." Explains Amar Singh Thakur, Kanhaal, Peontra.

The beauty and silence of Ghasnot pasture provides us a permanent romantic overtures to those opting for honeymoon in the Ghasnot. The night life in Ghasnot is full of liveliness and enjoyment. The days and nights are full of peace, serenity and calmness. The heart beats up cheerfully when we hear the sounds of the insects, wild birds or wild animals from a nearby distance. In the company of friends there is no fear while in the night. Some times the wild foxes weep in the dark of night and create amazing sounds.

The evening and morning in the high mountain pastures is a beautiful experiences and with memorable moments of life. The youths must enjoy such experiences in the wild of Chanshal.

Tangankha Pasture: Tangankha Pasture is amazing one and is called the Paradise of Gaddis. Gaddis arrive in summer and enjoy day and night life here. They cook food, sleep into a temporary shelter and recite many stories in day and night camping. They sing local folk songs and remember their youthful days of the past. Sometime they spend months in the pasture, they face sun, rain and winter amidst the pasture with their sheep and goats.

Tangankha Pasture is called the trekkers holiday home. In some way, it is the grazers paradise. The local Gaddis and Gujjars spend some days here during summer and remain there untill there is some heavy snowfull. The herds of the Gujjars and Gaddis leave for the warm valleys and plain region where they find shelter upto March.

In the month of April May they proceed on to mountain pastures and remain there when the whole of snow has melted away. Tangankha pasture is mostly known for the bright wild flowers, aromatic plants, and the wild grass emitting sweet smell from the flowers and roots. The whole pasture provides us a scented smell which sometimes makes us unconscious.

Tangankha Pasture is also called "Scholars Paradise" as every year the scholars from far away come here to trek the mountain peaks and camp in the open pasture. The place is beautifully located. It is considered the most enjoyable place for the poets, writers, academicians and those perceive for creative writing in the peace. The camp life is most enjoyable both in night and day time for domestic as well as outsiders.

Jangla-Ansar Valley: If we enter Jangla-Ansar Valley it turns into amazing world of trees, plants. herbs, shrubs and dwarf bushes. It is a paradise in itself. If we spend some nights and days in the Jangla-Ansar Valley it is more pleasant. It is a place mostly liked by the Gaddis of Himachal as they call it the wonder world of their life. The place is known among the trekkers and naturalists from far and near. During summer days, the valley turns into a peaceful paradise. The environment is warm and pleasant. Some cold waves deters our work. The wild flowers and aromatic plants are useful for medicinal purpose. This fragrance sometimes makes us feel the newcomers giddy and make him unconscious for a while. It is a nice experience while trekking through the valley of fragrance. Sweet scented air in the Jangla Ansar Valley "the scented smell of clay and wild grass fills our mind with pleasure and happiness. It is an experience to enjoy life into a beautiful pasture which provides newcomers the gifts of nature'. Who have already enjoyed the camplife in this strange valley. The camplife, dark nights and moon-lit nights are full of mysteries in nature and provides, many creative thoughts and ideas to many men and women.

The green landscapes of Jangla Ansar Valley are quite strange and amazing. This has provided us bitter experiences of life in this remote part of earth. This has filled all of us with a new enthusiasm and happiness to fight against the natural calamities and to become more confident in our efforts to enjoy life in the mountains.

There are some strange natural lands known for their ecological values. Some of the naturalists say that Jangla Anshar Valley is the larger one and has all the natural charms to attract the people from far and away. It has a vast plant kingdom of its own. It is an amazing world of rare plants, trees, medicinal herbs, alpine grass and wild flowers scattered in the nature. Covering the mountain peaks, slops and valleys, the alpine flowers have their particular characteristic.

Dodraa Quaar: Dodraa and Quaar are the most ancient villages of Himachal Pradesh, almost cut up from the rest of the hill region. They are situated far away in the wilderness where they are fully covered by snowfall for eight months. The ancient tradition, architecture, culture and patterns of the houses exist here and explains the artistry of ancient period. The houses are based on traditional patterns and bear the symbol of some Gods or Goddesses. The people celebrate almost every fair, festival and rituals in villages. They are emotionally attached to their religious sentiments and worship local Gods and Goddesses.

Dodraaa - Quaar is surrounded by beautiful mountain pastures and valleys. It is a tehsil in the outskirts of Chanshal valley some 42 kilometer from Larot. Although, Larot is linked to Tikri, Chirgaon via Dhamwari but Dodraaa Quaar still awaits for a pucca link road. The people almost visit the area on horse back or by trekking on foot. They bring ration and other useful articles from Chirgaon on their back. During snowfall the whole area is totally cut up from the rest of the Shimla District.

The culture and civilization of Dodhra-Quaar is said to be 2000 years old. They call themselves the children of Pandavas of Mahabharat period and require proper conservation for their culture through the Government and non-government organisations. The intellectuals, researchers, scholars, journalists environmentalists and botanists should visit such places of historical and geographical importance and write about their unique social and cultural heritage.

There is a great need to encourage eco-tourism activities for the socio-economic development of the people. There are great possibilities of Rural tourism in the area.

Dodraaa-Quaar is a place of natural peace, beauty, creativity and relaxation. It has become a popular destination for nature, wilderness and bird witching in this remote area. We should protect its ancient cultural heritage. The social studies departments in the universities and colleges should encourage the studies heritage, wildlife, trekking expeditions in Chanshal and other parts of the country. The people of Dodraa-Quaar are sincere, hard working and honest and are adapted to the hardships of life.

The people are more reliable and honest towards social life. They have a peculiar adherence and awareness towards their cultural heritage. The fares and festivals are full of religious sentiments. They worship their Gods and Goddesses with great faith and rejoice. The people celebrate their festivals and social events with great fanfare.

The modern youth is getting away from their cultural values. The government agencies should do their best to protect the unique cultural heritage of this ancient village. The people should be encouraged towards their cultural heritage and ancestral traditions to preserve it for a longer period. The coats, pattis, shawls, socks, shoes, pants and caps are made of sheep wool and are used by the villagers in the winter. When there is heavy snowfall, they wear heavy woolen coats to protect themselves from cold.

12

The Misty Mountains of Shivalik

The Shivaliks are made up of the eroded matter from the rising Himalaya. These are also called sub Himalayas with an average height of 900 to 1,200 meters. These are new fragile and small mountains.

A mountain range in the Shivalik Hills remain misty in every season and hence are called the misty mountains. The moisture generated by forests and local rivers make them misty all the times, particulary in rainy season and winter.

Dehradun is surrounded by the most fascinated Shivalik hills. The foot hills, river banks, pasture land and vastly expanded wilderness are full of adventure and are enjoyable for camplife at night. Shivalik hills dotted with giant bushes and trees are a home for violent wild animals like tigers, leopards, elephants and wild pigs.

The most impressive forests and wilderness lie in Rajaji National Park, near Motichur in "Raiwala." Kanshron forest range, Toya river orchid forests and the Saung river banks are a heaven for trekking, sight seeing, adventure skills, fishing and night life camping. These places remain full of mist and fog during rain and winter.

Camplife in the months of winter and summer is most enjoyable for the lovers of outdoor life. The camping beside the passing river is the most enjoyable activity for the students, teachers, parents and regular trekkers.

The river banks are neat and clean and full of greenery, shining sands and beautiful pebbles. It becomes creative and enjoyable for the adventure lovers to play with pebbles. Camping near the passing clean water is most enchanting and enjoyable recreation.

The Shivalik hills are quite rich in wild life *i.e.* tiger, elephants, ant bear, langoors, monkies, deer, Marsh deers are some of the mammals found in the Shivalik hills. Among the reptiles black snake, green snake and dotted back snake and python, are quite common. Among the bird fauna, kingfisher, huppoe, woodpecker, yellow bird, horn bill, koel, Hilansh, honey bird, peacock, turtle dove, crane, fish eater, skylark, chakor and wild fowls are found quite abundantly in the wild of Rajaji Park in Deharadun. Other strange animals, birds, insects, honey bees and butterflies are found here in the wild or wilderness.

Saung River: The Saung is a beautiful river but turns into a devastating floods during heavy rains. In many ways the river is a boon to local people as it provides them a lot of vegetables, medicinal plants, herbs and clean water. The river functions as a wet land to domestic animals and the inhabitants in nearby villages. All the wild animals and bird fauna found in Rajaji Park are depend on this clean water river. During winter, we can spot a row of white cranes on the banks of the river.

Sang River Water: Local, summer cranes are also found in the river bank near the forest land. The river provides a natural cooling system to the local inhabitants of the area. The water is crystal clear hence an ideal place for swimming. It is also useful for white water rafting and fishing. For fishing in a particular zone the local authorities may be contacted for the legal permission. There are five types of rare fishes in the waters of local rivers including Saung.

The bank of Saung river is a boon for the travellers, trekkers, botanists, environmentalists and explorers from the domestic as well as foreign lands. The main attraction is of the enchanting banks of the river and the wilderness of "Kansharon" near the Rajaji National Park (Motichur, Raiwala and Childderwala)

This place has a very beautiful swamp area for the studies of a aquatic flora and fauna. The varieties of aquatic plants, giant bushes, large trees, creepers, wild flowers. medicinal plants and tea flavour bushes also attract the foreign botanists, nature lovers and explorers with a great extent. The place can be developed for eco-tourism activities. This region has been a popular destination for trekking and exploration activities.

During spring season, the river bank turns into a heaven for explorers and botanists. We can sense sweet fragrance from the wild flowers and acquatic plants. The night and day camping near Saung river is quite delightful. It is like to enjoy life in a peaceful paradise.

The wilderness through Saung river is quite rich in bird fauna. The other wild animals like tigers, elephants, wild pig, python and other species of strange reptiles are found here. It is an amazing world in itself. We should explore the world of Saung river and wilderness with great enjoyment.

Orchid Forests-Toya River: The orchid forests of Chidderwala are known to the orchid lovers of the world. The most beautiful and most fragile orchids grow on the old trees of Toya river in Chidderwala. The terrestrial orchids grow over the land in Shivalik foothills. The Toya river marshland is an outstanding example of two epiphyte orchids with rare combination of humidity and epiphytes. The orchids are of two species

1. Vanda Cristata
2. Obenoria.

Vanda Cristata is found in the large saal trees and obenoria Mahua trees, Jamun trees and other relevant old trees in the marshland. Obenoria is a rare orchid species in the area. Both the species are on the verge of extinction due pollution, global warming and continuously decreasing marshland.

Hundred years ago, the forest land was spread up to more than sixty square kilometer but now it has been reduced to 3 or 4 kilometers respectively. One century ago the area was completely a swamp forest zone. In the year 1911, it was reduced upto 60 square km.

Toya river, a wetland is nature's peaceful paradise with several aquatic species both vegetables and herbs with medicinal values. There is a great need to protect and expand the area of wetland in the periphery of Toya river. The International Institute of Mountain Studies and Research (NGO) and Global Village (NGO) New Delhi have done their best to arouse public opinion for the protection of orchid forests. The parents, teachers associations (PTA) and schools and colleges have done their best to protect and conserve the orchid forests of Toya river in Chidderwala - Toya region.

The orchid flowers during October-November and this is the most auspicions season for the environmentalists and explorers to visit the marsh wetland. This is the best place of its kind in the rigion. The aquatic food vegetables and the fresh water mangroves are an attraction to the lovers of nature and wild plants.

The Kansher Wilderness: Kansher is a beautiful wilderness and forest cover near the Rajaji National Park in Chidderwala village of Doiwala Block in District Dehradun, Uttaranchal. Kansher is amazing wilderness with abound natural beauty. It is the paradise for explorers and trekkers. The forestland is spread upto several kilometers making it one of the dense and most popular wildland for the nature exploration activities. The plains of Saung river base, the river banks and the wide pastures in the vicinity create a beautiful scene for the nature lovers.

The sunsets and sunrise at the Saung river banks are quite bewildering. This creates a marvellous scenic views in the evening as well as in the morning. The trekking can be enjoyed in winter as well as in summer. The winter days are cold and harsh while the summer days are pleasant and full of nature's beauty. But for those who love to fight with challenges of life, the winter days are full of thrill with new ambitions of camplife. The winter camp can be organised near the bank of the river or the wide pasture land above the river bank. The tea, coffee and hot, fresh food can be enjoyed during the days and nights of the camplife.

The Joy of Spring Season: The vast stretch of Kansher forest is full of large trees. Some trees are quite dwarf and some are big in height. Most of the trees are dotted closely. When the spring season arrives the whole environment turns into a heaven of wild flowers and greenery. Every bud is in tender state and every blade of grass appears young as if the earth's cover is replanted with trees, wild flowers and long grass. The whole environment appears into a new romance of spring. The birds chirp sweet songs, the honey bees buzz and the wild fowls make some cautious sounds in the lap of nature. The wild flowers invite the colourful butterflies into the most impressive way. It seems as if the whole planet has been changed into a new world of wonderful natural beauty. The Kansher forests are known for its rich bird fauna. When the spring arrive the whole bird community chirp very sweet songs and make the environment more colourful and pleasant.

The Nesting of Birds in the Wild: The Kansher forests are covered by evergreen trees and bushes. The huge trees, dwarf bushes and spiral plants are known for their growth and the use of their tendrils which remain stick to the trees. The bushes are large and awesome. Some of the bushes are full of wild fruits, flowers and insects and are an ideal heaven for the birds as they get enough food for themselves. The activities of the wild birds become more energetic and they remain busy locate ideal places for their nesting. For example, they search out a safe bush, tree cavities and wall cavities. The cavities are mainly used by huppoe, king fisher, wood pecker and podeena birds. These are the most interesting birds in the forests. To watch their activities and locate their nests is an interesting hobby.

Kansher forests are full of different species of trees, plants and bushes. It is an ideal heaven for the nesting for birds. It takes time to locate safe and proper tree or bush for making nests. When the birds are fully confident about their safety and location, they prepare their nests, in the nearby bush or tree. The birds are of all types and make the nests on the bushes and trees of their choice. Some birds make their nests on fruit trees and some flowering bushes. Some birds on dry safe bushes. The small birds like Surady, pisty and tailor birds make their nests on the leafy bushes. They sew the leaves of bushes into a pouch and lay their eggs their in soft grass nests.

Rich Bird Fauna : The vulture, eagle and buzzard are the prey birds of Kansher forests. They make their nests on the long trees at the height of 60-70 feet from the ground. Their nests are as big as an umbrella. These nests are hugely prepared with the threads, ropes, iron, copper wire, wooden figs and various items like katora, soaps, human hairs, plastic bags, polythenes, large grass, sticks, gold chains, silver chains and various other items like animal bones, flesh and large parts of snakes etc. To watch the nests of vultures and eagles is full of excitement in itself and an amazing world of strange things. It is a big recreation and it takes several days to study and survey the nests of the vulture and eagle. Both are the prey birds and always hunt for small birds and their kittens. The bulbul, mouse birds, red finch, and black finch are the small song birds and depend on the local bushes for their nesting. These birds also survive on the small fruit bushes. Besides this, wild fowls, water fowls, red crow, white cranes, water cranes, Jungle flame, yellow singer, koel, kafoo, hilansh, hanshod, ronu (laughing birds and weeping birds), brown bird, black hornbill, skylark and turtle dove are found here. Some 85 wild birds some of them are beautiful song birds are found in the Kansher wilderness.

Nature Watching: Nature exploration and nature watching are two ideal hobbies for those who love and like the importance of nature into daily life. The beauty of nature has always been attracting the human minds. Whether they were the nature lovers, poets, writers and explorers, the nature has been making them the slave of her enchantment. The mountain peaks, valleys, slopes, river banks, pastures, forests, grasslands and wilderness have always been a source of attraction. This has been recreating and fascinating the human mind with their beauty and enchantment. The people from far and wide come to travel natural landscapes of Himalayan states of India. The most important place of natural beauty is Himalayan paradise, Nepal. Nepal is the heaven of richest, enchanting landscapes in the world. Even USA and Switzerland remain failure in comparison to Nepal. Nepal is a poor country in the world but is known for its richest natural resources. It is said that USA is having an eye to loot the natural resources of Nepal. The massacre of Royal family of Nepal is seen in this context.

The Bird Life and Wild Animals: The Kansher forests are known for its richest bio-diversity in Asia. The fauna and flora have its own strangeness, beauty and charm. First of all it is famous for Asia's largest mammals (1) Asian Elephants (2) Tigers (3) Leopards (4) Wild cow (5) Shivalik Deers (6) The Marsh deers (7) Wild boar (8) Monkies (9) Langoors (10) Brown foxes and (11) Bears. These are among the main large mammals of Kansher forests of Dehradun District. The reptiles are also found in different shapes and sizes (1) Python (2) Black snake-king cobra (3) Diamond back (4) Brown snakes (5) Green snakes (6) Black-brown snakes (7) Black-white dots on the back of it. (7) The water snakes found in the local rivers, wetlands and tanks are common.

The Avi Fauna (Bird fauna) of Kansher forests is quite amazing and full of bird species and most of them song birds. Particularly several bird species found near the swamp area. among them are : the swamp cranes, water fowls, wild fowls, brown river birds, horn-bill, kafoo, koel, yellow singer, kingfisher and several other beautiful birds (nearly 85 species of birds) are found in the Kansher range alone. The pastures, river banks and dense bushes are the best breeding grounds for the birds. During spring and winter these areas are natural inhabitation for the wild birds. Here bird watching camps can be organised by taking the permission from the Director of Rajaji National Park in Deharadun. The area is quite pleasant, warm and full of enchantment.

13

Baheli : An Ancient Forestland

Baheli Forests: If you remember Shakespeare's Garden of Nature, Baheli forestsland is a beautiful manifestation of that heavenly wild land. It is 20 km. from Pauri by bus and seven kilometers by trekking through the beautiful valleys. Baheli is an example of prime forests in the country. It is most enchanting wilderness envisaged for eco-tourism in the Pauri hills. It has a beautiful oak forests on moisturous part and on its temperate side, a well grown pine forest. The old pine forest is more than 200 years old and the man made forest is only thirty years old. The Oak and Rhododendran and Kafal (merica esculenta) trees have become scarce in this area. In ancient time, it was an amazing dense forest. The forests have a great importance for the people who love, enjoy and protect them. The geographical formation and structure of Baheli forestland is distinct and varied. During spring the forest land turns to a heaven for explorers and trekkers in the region. Some species of ferns and orchids grow here in the wild.

The most impressive aspect of the forest land is that it has become a model example of the flora and fauna in the area. The mountain tiger, bear, foxes, monkeys, rabbits and giant squirrel found in this area. Also rich in bird fauna. There are some 30 birds found in the forest land, wild fowls are common to spot. The teetar, chakor, blacklarge crow, karaoon, turtle dove, common dove, skylark, Red finch, black finch, Suradi, tailorbirds, mouse birds, yellow bulbul, black bulbul, flycacher, huppoe, chanchud and wild pigeon are found in the forests. The medicinal plants, aromatic herbs and wild flowers are the best source of botanical studies here.

Besides this, Baheli forestland is famous for several life-saving medicinal plants *i.e.,* Viola serpense (Vanaspa), Chiraita, ground cherry, rock-herbs, rock-rug, rock-ferns, lupia (edible herb) shaunshea (edible herb) and several other medicinal and ornamental plants are found in abundance.

Some ten species of terrestrial orchids and four species of lilies are found in the wilderness of Baheli, lily Gloriossa, lily wallichi, lily giant are found in the outskirts of Baheli. Baheli is a village known for its cultural heritage. This is among the oldest villages in the area where more than two hundred year old houses are found till to date; most of the houses are constructed with ancient cut stones. The oldmen and masons tell about the ancient cultural heritage and traditions. The people of the village are very hard working, peace loving and religious with spritual leaning. They worship local Gods and Goddesses. The village is situated in the valley at the height 3000′ and has a fertile land which grow food grains and vegetables abundantly for their requirements. It can become a model example of wilderness management and eco-tourism activities in the area. It is surrounded by a mixed forest land and linked with a bus route to district capital Pauri and the religious place Jwalpa Devi.

Wild Flowers: The wild flowers in the mountains of Shivalik range of terai region are most exciting and bright in colour and composition. Some of them are very strange, some very exotic and some quite amazing in quality and colours. It is very exciting when we pass through the valley of wild flowers in different parts of the Himalayas. For example, in Western Himalayas we remember our days spent in gloriously in Chanshal in Rohru, Pyuntra and Malana Valley in Chaupal. Some areas are quite famous for flowering pastures. The environmentalists, botanists, trekkers and explorers visit the valleys of flowers and explore the nature nurseries of wild flowers and alpine plants. The Western Himalayas includes Chanshal valley, Sangla valley, Natural Park, Kullu, Jubbal Kupped which are among the best examples of high attitude zone wild flowers.

Himachal Pradesh is the best example of Western Himalaya's natural nurseries *i.e.*, wild flowers, alpine plants, herbs, trees, ferns and moisture loving plants are found in the slopes and valleys. Pauri Hills are in the Shivalik range and are a beautiful example of mountains flowers. the mountain flowers found in

Western Himlayas are quite different from that of Shivalik range. In general, there is an amalgamation of Alpine, temperate and semi temperate wild flowers.

The wild flowers in Shivalik range vary from place to place. The upper heights, lower heights and foothills. valleys have a different combination of wild flowers and moisture loving plants. The temperate zones have different types of plants and moisturous zones have different wild flowers.

The Importance of Baheli: The village is situated in valley surrounded by Oak, cedar and pine forests. The people are good farmers and prepare shining nurseries of paddy and vegetables. Once the village was a model example of a self sufficient village in the area. Most of the population has settled down in cities and very few people live there now.

The Shivalik Himalayan Birds: The Shivalik Himalayan birds are rare and most beautiful in colour. Some of the species of birds live in middle Himalayan foothills.

Wild Birds: During winter some birds migrate from Western Himalayas to Middle Himalayas. The Shivalik range have rare bird fauna in the world. The breeding colonies of the birds, their habitats and alpine forests are a natural place of their existence. The old trees, wood cavities, rock cavities and traditional habitats of birds should be protected. A large number of them has been wiped out in the past one century. This has reduced the population of most of the beautiful mountain birds and wild fowls. Some most important trace birds are and Monal Pheasant, Western Himalayan Tragopan, Jaju Rana Cheer Pheasant, K. Wallichi, common wild fowls and the Ratnal.

Himalayan Granifora, Jajurana and other rare and important mountain birds are found in the area. The shivalik hills have some beautiful species of birds. Raucus crow, common crow, Hilansh, Kafoo, Koel, Red finch, Mouse bird, bulbul, yellow neck, Bulbul red neck, mountain sparrows, (two species,) skylarks (two species), crying bird, turtle dove, long tailed birds karoon and saroon are some of them. (Karaoon - light orange and saroon dark sky blue colour birds) are found at from 1000′ to 7000′ height. Mostly the blue magpie seen in the high hills, while red magpie is seen in the valleys. There are different birds at temperate and semi-temperate zones.

The pheasants like teeter, bater, chakor and other impressive birds are found in lower heights of the wilderness.

The Birds of Saung Forests: The mountains forests are quite popular breeding grounds for several species of wild fowls and colourful song birds. At the arrival of spring, the birds assemble in a forest and sing very sweet songs. The valleys are full of flowers and fruit trees during spring and birds assemble into the wet land and heathlands of the mountains. One such paradise of song birds is Giri Ganga in Kupped Wilderness Jubbal, Himachal. The other ideal places are in the Shivalik foothills in Toya river and Saung river wilderness in Uttaranchal. The birds chirp day and night and sing sweetest songs of life in the spring. The people, mostly trekkers and explorers enjoy life in the solitude of wilderness. The bird watchers and field ornithologists explore valleys to valleys in search of song birds and photograph them from a distance. It is quite sad that most of wild birds are disappearing from forests. Most of the wild flowers, bushes, fruit trees, and natural habitats has been destroyed by the local people and the enemies of the birds! Global warming, pollution and felling of old trees and bushes is also one reason of disappearing of birds.

We all the aware citizens of the world should protect wild plants, flowering bushes, wild fruit trees, and the natural habitats of birds and animals with our best efforts. The earth is our common homeland and we should protect it by all positive efforts.

The Tigers of Daaligaad:

The Shivalik Hills. The Daaligaad forestland is known for its natural beauty and varieties of plants, bushes and trees. It is considered among the medium range wilderness which are known for their rich bio-diversity. The wilderness has three types of ecosystem (1) The temperate zone facing the direct sun rays during summer as well as winter. The semi-temperate bushes, trees and plants are in multiple growth. Some of them wild fruit plants and useful bushes. The bushes are used as fuel, fodder and timber. (2) The long grass land, this is also a semi-temperate zone where the grass is used for the purpose of fodder by the villagers and is cut by the women every year in the winter. The whole area with the adjoining village forests is 10 square km and is enough for the grazing territory of village cattles. The forest area is controlled by village Panchayat and the grass and wood is distributed every year. (3) The third is moisturous zone. This is a combination of mixed forests, wild grass and Amla, Beheda, Timul trees in the valleys and some plain lands with slow water sources in the low lands. The down plain land is called "Talain" and plain upland. "Baadeyun" in the local language in Pauri Garhwal in Uttaranchal. The forest land is 22 kilometer from "Pauri", the capital city of Pauri Garhwal. The Talain area (also called Terain or plain land) has some cave like rocks, heavily dotted bushes, dark valleys and long grasses where it makes perfect hiding sites for leopard, mountain tigers, wild fowls, shahi, rabbit, mountain deers, jackals and foxes. The wild fowls and other birds, mammals, monkies and wild cats are found here. In the night, the tigers and leopards roam here and there in search of "prey" and during day time they rest into their caves or under the dark bushes.

The population of tigers in the mountain forests have increased ten fold since 1972 when the "Save the Asian Tiger Project" was first launched by the lovers of fauna and flora. It is said that in 1972, there were only two tigers one male and one female in the area (Daaligaad Tiger cave) but now there are at least twenty tigers in the surrounding of 20 sq. km. The village cattles are the target of their regular attack. The goats, sheep and cattles (cow, ox and bulls), from the nearby villages are killed regulary. Sometime the tigers come into the houses where the cattles live. From Gorindi, Patal, Paniya, Nausin "Jairam Ki Kooli", Simtoli, Jakhni, Maroda, Dhar ka Margaon, Molthi, Baheli, Srikot, Chorkandi and Kyard are regularly attacked by the bush tigers of Daali Gaad. There are two fatal locations of tiger inhabitation, one in Daali Gaad known as the caves of tigers (Baag Ki Tibari) and in the forest valley of "Dharka Margaon" and Molthi forest land. When the tigers or leopards do not find their prey in the forests they attack domestic animals in the outskirts of Daaligaad, Ghora Dhungi, Gaamaath, Shilwani, Talain and in and around of the above villages whenever the violent animal find the opportunity, the cattle is grabbed and killed at the spot. In Dhar Ka Margaon, the tiger has killed tree people in a month. Later on, the villagers got angry and surrounded the tiger and killed him through stones and sticks. The tigers in the local areas have become the instant killers for the local human population Whenever they do not find the wild animals for their prey in the forests, they come out towards villages and attack innocent human lives. Small children are their main target.

Wildlife Act: The killing of innocent human lives by the tigers has put a big question mark before the protectors of wild life! Should we be left free to die into the jaws of such violent animals? We have been protecting them for the past several decades and now they are our instant killers! Can we not kill the violent animals in our self defence if they are going to attack us! Are the human being more inferior than this violent animals? The human lives are negligible! And are the tigers more important than human lives? If somebody is going to kill the tigers in self defence, he is badly trapped under wild life protection act and put behind the bars as he has violated the wild life protection laws by killing this violent animal? Should we not revise our wild life laws which are centuries old? Should we not revise the old wild life laws which have become irrelevant in the modern age of science? These are some questions which are stirring the mind and body of the environmentalists, wild life experts, nature lovers and explorers.

We should make it more clear that the wild animals which are going to kill human lives should be killed immediately without any permission from the district authorities? We have several obstacles in the name of laws, taking permission it takes weeks and the wild animal slips away in another village territory to kill other innocent children, men and women? There is no life more important than the human life! We should protect the human life at any cost! The wild life and the forest department should ensure the safety of the human life living near the forests.

The Killer Tigers : The tigers of Daaligaad have killed so many cattles in the past four decades and the violent animals were not controlled by the wildlife laws? In the nearby villages, dozens of children either killed or maimed by the attack of tigers. Several innocent lives were killed in Chamoli Garhwal, Tehri Garhwal and Uttarkashi Districts in Uttaranchal. In Kumaon region we have been receiving several such stories, where the small children and women were made targets by the tigers and the bears. The bodies of the victims were badly tored or damaged by these violent animals. The man should create a fear into the hearts of such violent animals. They should be attacked instantly when they attack the human beings. The illegal hunting and smuggling of hides should be banned and the culprits should be punished.

In some villages of Chamoli Garhwal, the tigers were roaming in the villages fearlessly and in the evening entering the house and killing the men, women and the children. Sometime the village people are so scared that they live in acute fear and distress. This violent animal can attack the innocent people at any time after the dusk.

The Tigers of Daaligaad in Pauri Garhwal have increased in population and their fear still hunting the village people. The cattles are killed near the village forests and woodlands in the broadday light. The domestic cattles are being attacked regularly. To kill a domestic cattle mean a loss of Rs. 5000 to a villager. The poor man have no money to buy another cow, bull or ox. He has to face nature's scratches and the fear of this violent animal!

The humane question arises that we are the protector of wild life and are we on the mercy of violent animals? Should we not protect ourselves in self defence? When we wait for the DM's/ DFO's permission, the animal kills as many people as possible in the village surrounded by dense forests.

We should protect the wild life but we should not die like a dog into the jaws of violent animals! We should protect ourselves by any means. And we should know that we are not to die before wild animals!

We should follow wildlife Act, nature protection laws by all positive means but we should not die into the jaws of a tiger or any other violent animal.

The Floral Diversity: Daaligaad wilderness is rich in floral diversity. For example mini sunflower plants, Vanashpa (viola serpens), Lupia, Pather chatta, Leontopodium alpinum, Lisimachia Punctata, Troleus Himalayensis, larkspur, Varbasum longifolium, Kunja, giant lily, mountain lily, yellow orchids, white orchids, Mashal chana, Khaburshula, comb-orchids and Kamalia (Berenia ciliata) are found into the wild of Daaligaad. In many ways, Daaligaad is a heaven for medicinal herbs, aromatic plants, orchids and giant lilies. Lily wallichi is also found in the wilds of Daaligaad. There are at least five varieties of Lily wallichi or snake lilly. Some of them are found in the mountain peaks upto the height of 6000′-7000′ (temperate and moisturous place). The second type of lily is found within 4000-5000′ in the shade loving areas. The third type of lily is found near 3000-4000′ also moisturous or shade loving areas under the giant bushes.

Wild Flowers: Some speices of wild peas, wild lady's finger and wild cotton plants, Buglya-Anaphalis royleana, Saccharum spontanous lin, vetivenne zizoxiodes Nash are found in Daaligaad and wet plain lands. The names of such plants and herbs are available in the local languages. We have to do a lot of surveys and research work for the botanical classification of the plants, trees and bushes.

Exploration and Camp Life: Daaligaad is a heaven for ideal camp life and exploration activities. There are some small and big leeches in the wet lands of Daaligaad so one should be careful while drinking water near the water springs and wetlands. The presence of fish and leeches means the water contains some pollution. Also, the presence of various other bottom fauna indicates the impurity of the water. But there are many other sources of drinking water in the wild and we should take it from good one.

The Markhudee Woodlands

Markhudee is a beautiful barren land (wood land) in the interiors of Pauri Garhwal. The forest land is known for its amazing varieties of trees, wild grasses, growing plants, Jal Toonga, Toonga, Khaina (Ficus Auriculata) Timul (Timla), Bedoo (Phedoo) all from ficus family of trees and bushes. Besides this, the barren area is a marvellous example of a barren ecosystem in a semi-temperate area. This barren land is widely knwon as "Janaki Devi's Wood land."

There are some bushes of shulla, a mountain cactus which produces milky water and is applied in the itching part. This milky substance cures skin diseases also. The resin coming out of the shulla tree is quite harmful and is a toxin to the fishes. When the shulla leaves and stem is crushed into a paste and is left in the small rivulets. The fishes gets intoxicated by the paste and one can easily catch up those unconscious fishes.

Khinna is also a wild cactus tree and produces white resin when it is cut and is quite harmful toxin. It is also used to poison the fishes in the tanks and rivers.

Markhudee is spread upto 3 km^2 and is an ideal place for evening and morning visits just near the agricultural boundary of the Simtoli village. Markhudee is a rocky land with semi-temperate plants and herbs on it. Among the domestic trees are Khareek and Bheemal (also known as "Bhewnl"), produces popular leaf food for the cattles.

Comb-orchid is also found in this barren-land here. Purvat (Leontopodium alpinum) Lupia, Pathar chatta, wild grapes (Bherna), Genthee, Taidoo, Mashalchana, Khabarshula, wild lily and giant lily is found here in the wild of this wood land. Vanashpa: viola serpens is also found along with the other remedial herbs. The most amazing and important thing is that the Markhudee wood lands is a semi-temperate area and is a heaven for Bherna, the famous wild grapes. These grapes in the wild are considered God's indispensable gifts in nature! These grapes are very sweet, lovely and so much impressive to our eyes as they remain in beautiful bunches. It becomes more enjoyable when they turn black and are sweet in their peak seasons. A grape plant has at least 20-30 bunches of sweet grapes. This is an ideal food for birds, squirrel, and several other wild animals. The spiraling grape plant's beauty is much more enjoyable when it is full of bunches of fruits.

Markhudee: Pleasant for Summer as well as Winter Days: During sunny days of summer the Markhudee is quite pleasant and it provides peace, physical relief when we relax in the lap of wild land. When there is bright sun during winter days, we can enjoy sleeping over the warm grass in this peaceful paradise. We can prepare a "Gumtee" shelter here in the open pasture or at a place where we can enjoy the warmness of the land without facing any cold wave coming from the far away peaks. Here we can plan a natural study centre for ourselves to enjoy during winter as well as summer days.

The Pastures

The Open Pastures and Cool Breeze: It was the month of June when we travelled through the mountains and after heavy work load and trekking we had to take rest at Markhudee. It was bright sun and we were sweating heavily. With our team we laid down at an open pasture under the shadow of Khareek tree. It is also called by us as *"Bari Didi ka Khet"* which later on was left as barren land after her death. Here we took permanent rest for some days, the cool breeze was striking at our faces providing us complete relief from the scorching sun. Every person got perfect rest and we were refreshing ourselves for our next journey. Here we took the refreshment we had brought with us. From here, we went to Thanda Paani, Katraa Siaraa, Shilwanee and Gaad Paar areas where we enjoyed a lot of botanical plants, wild flowers and the aquatic plants.

Sleeping and Taking Rest: If we organise a camp for twenty days, Markhudee is the best place to take rest and enjoy sleeping as this place is without biting insects and mosquitoes. The environment is quite pleasant and the cool breeze always caresses our body with its special messages that be cool and happy everyday. The surrounding is full of multipurpose trees and bushes which are loving to observe. The place is full of leafy bushes and wild grass and also the song birds and wild fowls. The sweet chirping of birds in the morning and evening is a big recreation for all of us in the nature. It is not only a great recreation for the bird lovers but a beautiful research work for the ornithologists in the nature. There are habitats and natural surroundings of the birds. Some of the birds in Markhudee, Jameen Kholi, Gherya and in Chopdeun area sing sweetest songs and are in groups from mornings to evenings. The noise of chanchuds, karaoon (magpies) bulbul, mouse bird, black bird, red finch, black finch and white fly catcher are some of the birds which are known for the sweetest songs in the wild particularly during the time of bright sun. They sing very beautiful songs, always dear to the ears.

Beautiful Place for Observation: The woodland of Markhudee creates a very fascinating views during the summer as well as winter days. We can have a look from here to the nearby villages shining in the light of the sun. The local pastures Charaan and grasslands can be seen and trekked easily from this point. From this place we can see Baheli forest land, Jaspurkandai wilderness, Chaurnee Dhaar, Dooli Dhaar, Gendu Dhaar, part of Ghora Dhungee Dhaar, Gaamaath Dhaar, Achariyaan and a part of Nagarja Dhaar with beautiful angles of telescope. We can see without telescope also as the places are quite nearer to Markhudee. Through telescope we can see detailed parts of trees, plants and wild flowers. It is quite beautiful to observe the nature from very near and enjoy every moment of it.

A heaven for Wild Plants: Markhudee is a heaven for wild plants and dwarf trees. All the wild bushes, dwarf plants and ground plants (creepers) have a valuable medicinal importance to the people of this area. The plants, trees and ferns are useful for human life. Here the temperate fern is most common and can be used for botanical studies as no research work has been conducted on this mountain fern by now. The stem of this fern is round with golden hairy structures as if it was made in heaven. It is so impressive and beautiful in look that most of the botanists and environmentalists take it for their collection. This temperate fern is full of golden hairs at the stem and is an asset for the botanists and fern lovers.

This fern is also known as "Fairy's head". Its stem is head like structure and full of golden hairs. This makes a very beautiful collectible items in the Pauri Hills. There are six more ferns in the area which grow in the temperate or semi-temperate regions where there is moisture but sun rays also dominate the area during bright sun. One single leaf (blade fern) fern is also found here. Some other ferns are moisture loving ferns and are found in the deep of colder valleys. But these are good ornamental ferns and found near Panchoo ka Chuya. There is one variety of dragon fern which is found at the height of 6000′ near the large bushes in the shady environment. It is found in the groves of Nagarja Dhaar. The edible ferns (linguda) is found near the banks of very small rivers in the area.

Markhudee is most popular place for the growth of red fern in the area. This place is a heaven for small botanicals. The ferns, moss, riccia and marcantia are found in the moisturous place here. This makes a beautiful place for the studies of botanical plants, medicinal herbs and large domestic trees used in fodder like Khareek and Bheemal, Malu, Gweeral. Earlier, Markhudee woodland was a heaven for densely populated trees like Khareek, Bheemal, Painya, Timla, Bedoo, Gweeral, Oak and pine, Sanwala (Toonga) and Jal Toonga but it has been denuded by the antisocial elements, mostly local people who live near the woodland. Some have damaged this land with their harmful attitude towards the nature. The woodland, if managed properly can become an ideal source for food, fodder fuel and timber. The wood land is Janaki Devi's property and her family members enjoy that wild land. The people from far and near come to study the botanicals in the area. The place is an ideal one for bird watching.

The Janaki Devi's wood land, once was a heaven for wild birds, rabbits, foxes, wild fowls, huppoe, turtle dove, mouse bird, bulbul, white and grey skylarks, black bird Kaljeenth, Karaoon, Saraoon (also known as Karain and Sarain), the red finch, black finch (both of them are song birds the black finch is always found in the wild land of Kingora, Hissaloo and Toonga bushes. The reason is because the bushes provide sweet fruits during summer and the birds enjoy them. When there are no insects, they survive on these fruit bushes. During the summer days, April-May-June the birds have their nesting period and chirp very sweetly. The song birds sing their sweet songs and the bird watchers have very-very enjoyable days in Markhudee, Shilwanee, Kataraa Siaraa, Gaad Paar, Naagadana, Gheraa, Goginee, Godiun and other places of bird inhabitation. The trees, bushes and dwarf plants are in plenty and the people enjoy their days in the valleys and pastures by collecting woods, fodder and timber. These places are ideal for bird watching, photography and camping in the wild. The days are more romantic and full of peace and natural beauty.

Ideal for Exploration and Camplife: Markhudee is nature's lovely place during the summer days when there is full spring and the beautiful birds chirp sweet songs into the wild. The environment is full of peace and serenity and the cool breeze always strike over our face. This provides us a lot of respite during summer days.

The Open Pastures: There are some agricultural fields which have been turned into open pastures for the past three decades. These fields turned pastures have been an ideal ground for relaxing in the sun. The sun is bright warm during the winter and the grass is a dry bed cover and provides ample energy and comfort into the open sun. The surrounding bushes provide us an ideal cover and shelter from the winter winds.

The summer days are most enjoyable both for camplife as well as trekking through the wild. We can locate very beautiful sites for nature watching as well as bird watching, in the nearby open fields, valleys, ravines and barren rock lands.

The place is most enjoyable, and protective, for camplife we can trek from this place to four directions.

1. We can trek to Baheli-Chorkandi valleys and pastures also locate the temples of their Devi Devta. Local Gods and Goddesses and their anthropological studies.
2. From Markhudee it is most challenging and enjoyable to ride *Jaspur Kandai* mountains and cross the lower forests upto Molthi and Ayaal forest land. Here, we can enjoy several water streams and water springs in the lower river valleys.
3. Markhudee is an ideal base camp for our relaxation point from where we can approach to Ghora Dhungee pasture and forest land, Kataraa Siaraa, Shilwanee, Thanda Paanee and we can explore "Linguda" and "Papadee" wild vegetables near the small rivers from Bhara Dhandee to Godiyoon upto Haidee Dhar. If necessary, we can visit the forest land of Baheli. This oak tree forest is among the most recreative ancient forest lands. The Oak tree forest is a boon to the Baheli village. The back side of it is full of pine tree. It gives a very beautiful impressions. The Oak forest is useful for generation of water sources for the village. That's why after 300 meters down the mountain, the sweet water spring sparkles. This mineral water in Baheli village is, sweet, cold and pure for drinking. The water source

is generaled in that place because of the ancient growth of oak trees. From here, we can complete one day tour and can visit various mountain peaks, forests, pastures, and rivulets emerging out from the lap of nature. We can visit Molthee, Shrikot and Dhar Ka Margaon Koladee, Jaspur Kandai and Simtoli villages where the forests are very close to the villages. Here, we can locate several bird sites and nesting areas and can have detailed photography amidst the nature.

The Scenic Wild Lands and Wild Flowers : During spring days and after the rain the mountains of Pauri hills are full of liveliness. The exciting bright mountain flowers, new buds coming out from the plants, trees and herbs display a beautiful glimpse. The wild lands and pedestrian path sides remain full of multi colour flowers. Karhatu (dandelion) Taraxacum officinabhlis weber, Chireta showy swertia (swertia speciosa D.Don 3000 meters), Senecio crysan the moides DC (2500 meters), Semper vivum acuminatum Decue (3000 meters), Saussurea taraxacifolia wall. (3000 meters), Sedum ewersii ledeb, succulent perennial herbs (2500 meters), chaula (Himalayan Balsam Policeman's helmet (Inpatients glandula fera Royle, (2500 meters), Spurred gentian (Halenia elliptical D.Don. (2500 meters), Ratanjot (shepherd's needle) Geranium wallichianum D.Don and sweet (2000 meters), meen (Arisaema Costatum (wall). Mart ex-scott (2000 meters) also called sarp dansh pen; Buglya (Royle's Anaphalis) Anaphalis royleana (2500 meters) Buglya (Anaphalis cuneifolia hook) (3000 meters), Rhododendron barbatum (During snowmelt (2500 meters), Buransh (Rhododendron arboreum (1500 meters), Buras Vanashpa (Viola Serpens) (2000 meters), Lark Spur (4000 meters), Lisimachia Punctata (2300 meters) Feunladi, Bhamakoo (Varbascum longifoliam (2000 meters), Liliam himalayensis, Purvat (Leontopodium alpinum) comb orchid white horse (1000 meters), snow flower orchid (500 meters) are some of the rare mountain flower. Baheli wild land, Nagarja, Jaspur Kandai and Daaligaad remain full of orchids and other striking mountain flowers. The beauty and glamour of earth increases much more while trekking over the large chunks of prestine wild lands.

14

Rampur Bushahar : An Ancient City of Traders

Rampur Bushahar is an ancient city of traders situated at the beautiful bank of Satluj. Rampur Bushahar has been a place of cosmopolition culture, goodwill and social harmony from the very ancient time. Established on the bank of Satluj river it provides a beautiful panoramic view in the morning as well as evening from its famous mountain top airport. It is an excellent helipad-cum-airport for the domestic tourists and VVIPS of the country.

The surrounding of Rampur Bushahar is not only peaceful and enjoyable but full of natural beauty. The city is a bustling busy tourist destination with several beautiful streets to enjoy the variety of market. It provides enough knowledge on its topography and fertile orchards. In some pockets, it has marvellous rangeland and heath land to enjoy the beautiful birds. Here, we can witness some manmade forests. Reforestation of eucalyptus and pine trees is quite visible from the far and near of the road sides. The marvellous architecture of Padam Palace and its surrounding impresses us the most. The people from far and near come to see Padam Palace among the travellers from foreign countries. It has become a place of great attraction among the international travellers. The Palace reveals several historical stories imbibed with the honesty and sincerity of Raja Padam Singh, the great ruler of Rampur Bushaher and Sarahan.

The scattered apple orchards, vegetable farms and green forest patches are a great attraction to all of us. Rampur Bushahar is ahead in the cultivation of apple and food vegetables. Proper attention is paid in the cultivation of apple in Rampur Bushahar and adjoining regions. The people are rich and royal because of their cash crops.

The landsslide occurs during rainy days. Sometime, the Satluj takes a devastating turn during the heavy rain in the area. Rampur is a bustling mountain city and is an image of the memory of past and present of the erstwhile Rampur Bushahar State. It has some of the very beautiful ancient temples, the traditional houses and Palaces. The Padam Palace is the main focus of tourists attraction. The lower Bazar is a busy one and can be termed as a complete market from a tourists point of view. In summer, Satluj flows quietly through its natural serpentine course and its skyblue water, impresses us a lot. The flow of the river water provides us a sweet music to our ear.

It is quite amazing that after a century, Satluj river took a devastating turn in the heavy rain of August 2000 in which 21 bridges including the 100 year old Victorian Bridge were flown away in the flood. A large number of shops, houses and lives were destroyed. In the morning of August 1 at 3.50 a.m. the Satluj turned into a dreaded deluge and the flood touched upto 10.5 meters scale and almost vanished away everything whatever came into the way. The main bridges of the town were washed away in a swing of flood. The deluge has caused much damage to the houses, men, women and animals. The land was swept away on the night of 31 July or 1st August morning at 3.50 a.m. 2000. It was 3.30 when the river water crossed the small bridges and swept away them within half an hours. The speeding and devastating flow of the river turned its course more violent. There was no chance for the people to save themselves. The water currents took away several lives as around 25 persons were flown away as their bodies were found more than twenty kilometers away from the spot. It was a more sentimental and tearful scene in the disrupted and devastated Rampur.

The river Satluj has given a timely warning to those who have played wrong with the nature. The people and their houses were in badly damaged and it will take time and money to relocate the resources and manage the construction properly. The famous Lakshmi Narain temple on the bank of the river swept away along with its pillars, only a few small parts, of it are existing at the present site. The construction work was going on with the co-operation of every community and their volunteers. The people had faced an irreparable loss in the history of this devastating flood in Rampur.

The river bank of Satluj are narrow with dreaded turns of the water course. It is quite sad that everything was washed away within seconds and without any early warning of flood in day time. The flood remained for fifteen minutes and washed away everything tragically.

It is revealed by the villagers and city dwellers that the deluge of August 1 at 3.30 am at night when the people were asleep into their houses, the river banks were alive with the street vendors, vegetable sellers as they had slept at the dark of night. All of a sudden they were swept away with the waves of the speeding water of Satluj.

The river was in its full swing and the heavy stones, sands, concrete, pebbles were flown away into a jolting speed. Three bridges on the river surrounding of Rampur town were swept away. The oldest bridge of Victorian period which was constructed in 1901 was also swept away by the devastating flood. The people are aware and cynical about the rage of Satluj in the coming rainy seasons. It never went like this as on August 1, 2000. The river rose into a very deceitful way.

Rampur Bushahar is trekkers paradise. Most of the trekkers trek through the banks of Satluj or through the silk routes of high mountains. The exploration activities along the bank of Satluj are much more enjoyable and adventure loving.

Rampur Bushahar is considered among the largest states of Himanchal Pradesh which has its own sources, fertile land, beautiful apple orchards and a rich socio-cultural life. The people are more religious, honest and co-operative in nature.

The Sarahan Palace, orchards, Mata Bheemakali temple, and most enjoyeble bird sanctuary are some of the prominent places for the trekkers, explorers and the class one tourists to visit this ancient capital of Rampur Bushahar State.

Rich Cultural Heritage: Rampur Bushahar is known for its rich cultural heritage. The temples, houses and the ancient architect, fairs and festivals and the generosity of its beautiful and sincere people.

The largest helipad in the shape of aerodromme is consturcted in Rampur Bushahar from where we can fly to any part of the region. A medium size plane can fly and get down at the helipad. The place is surrounding by the most enchanting mountains and forest lands.

Activity of Business Men: Rampur Bushahar has a cordial environment for the business class as well as medium class travellers in the area. The hotels, bars, cafes are well designed and decorated in modern fashion. The Himachal tourism has given them a good shape for attracting more tourists from foreign lands. For trekkers and travellers, there are cheap and best restaurants, guest houses and private hotels also. Besides this, other Government rest houses and accommodation is available here on reasonable rates.

During tourist season, it is very difficult to get space in a restaurant and a guest house. In some way, you will have to remain a paying guest in a friends house or a local resident of the area. In this way, your interests will remain more safe and workable and you will get a peace loving family environment to enjoy life afresh.

City of Temples: Rampur Bushahar has a great row of ancient temples to enjoy religious life. There are some newly construct temples in Rampur Bushahar.

At day, you can visit the Palace, the ancient temples and a well planned hospital, Raghunathji temple the magnificent helipad, the cool blue water of Satluj and the other side of Rampur Bushahar, the village, people, their customs and traditions with a broad - based anthropological studies are a memorable experiences of life.

SARAHAN: HEAVEN OF WESTERN HIMALAYAS

Sarahan is the nature's peaceful paradise. It is a real heaven in Western Himalayas. It is trekkers and explorers paradise.

Sarahan is the most enjoyable place to visit during summer days. It can prove an extra adventure spirit if we trek and camp here during snowfall also. This is the most romantic place in Rampur where we can enjoy four seasons of the year. Here we can visit the Palace, most ancient temple of Goddess Bhimakali, a air castle helipad, playground and the wild bird breeding centre are the best options for us. Sarahan is a bird watchers paradise. It has the most enchanting wilderness. The place is a model example of eco-tourism activities. The religious tourists throng here every year. The people have great faith in Mother Goddess Bheemakali and other deities and come here to perform Puja ceremony from far and wide. Mother Bheemakali is the most popular goddess of Himachal Pradesh.

Sarahan is the most beautiful place in Himachal Pradesh as it is surrounded by a beautiful foresr cover and mountain peaks. It is situated at 9,500 and has famous wild bird sanctuary with 144 birds and a suitable staff to look after it. Sarahan is some 25 km from Jeori and Jeori is 45 km from Rampur Bushahar. Here is the world famous temple of mother Bheemakali, the Great Goodess in Mahabharat age. The people come to worship and celebrate the festivals of Mother Godders from Delhi, Bombay, Chennai, Bangalore, Calcutta, Ahamedabad and various other parts of the country. The people get peace of mind, a life long pleasure of worship ceremony and an immense pleasure of Sarahan's natural beauty.

This is also the family Goddess of Raja Virbhandra Singh, former Chief Minister and most celebrated leader of Himachal Pradesh. The American and British writers have put him among the most popular leaders of the masses.

The whole Sarahan is nature's peaceful paradise and is surrounded by kail and cedar trees. The highest peak of Sarahan is above 11.000 and the facing peak Srikhand is 18000: Srikhand Mahadev is the highest peak in the area and has become quite popular among the explorers and adventure lovers of the country.

Religious Tourism: Sarahan is quite famous for its religious sentiments and fairs and festivals. The people are religious and peace loving, sincere and honest in day to day affairs.

Emotionally, they are attached with the Mother Goddess. They participate in the regious affairs and festivals.

Sarahan Palace: The Sarahan Palace is the oldest one and most magnificent in the area. It was constructed more than 150 years back during British Raj. The appearance and architecture of the palace and its enchanting surrounding is most enjoyble and peace loving.

Adventure Tourism: Himachal Pradesh is a heaven for adventure tourism. It has played a marvellous role in encouraging eco-tourism in the region. Hence ecotourism, wildlife sanctuary and adventure tourism are co-related. The most significant is the Wild Bird Sanctuary in Sarahan which attracts thousands of pilgrims every year.

There is a great importance for Eco tourism activities in a natural place like Sarahan. There is a good combination of nature tourism, religious tourism, and wild bird sanctuary.

1. Conservation Activities: Outstanding scenery, a wonderful climate and a wealth of adventure options make Himachal Pradesh unique eco-tourism distination. To ensure the survival of vulnerable wild life species, ecosystems, protection of huge tracts of pristine wilderness which provide a shelter to a wealth of mountain fauna and flora.

2. Great Outdoors: Himachal's natural areas provide shelter to mountain Pheasants and other song birds in the wild. Sarahan is a God's own land and a natural habitat for Monal Pheasant (Lophorus Impejanus) Jaju Rana (Western Himalayan tragopan) and other important mountain birds including. Kaleej pheasant. The Sarahan based Wild Bird Sanctuary has 144 wild birds from western Himalayan environment. This wild bird sanctuary is famous worldwide.

Tourism makes a vital contribution to the protection and conservation of these reserves (as well as the rehabilitation of damaged areas) by promoting awareness of value of nature and creating political pressure to conserve natural resourses. Tourism also provides to maintain wild life populations and habitats, more job creations, influx of foreign currency and capital investment, for the promotion of trekking and tourism.

3. Eco-tourism: Eco-tourism is loosely defined as the preservation of eco tourism, historical sites and indigenous cultures where benefits from tourism are passed onto local people is playing a vital role in the economic growth and development of our country.

Eco-tourism industry plays a vital role in the democratisation of society by developing human resources for the promotion and development of the people in various areas of tourism.

4. Sarahan : A Heaven: We have already mentioned that Sarahan is a heaven for eco-tourism activities. Sarahan (31°31′N, 77°48′E) is about 176 km from Shimla and 80 km from Rampur. In the Satluj valley Sarahan is situated at the height of 9,500 meters. This place is known as the abode of Goddess Bheemakali's and ancient capital of Rampur Bushahar, one of the largest princely states in the Shimla hills. Sarahan is a popular destination or explorers and trekkers of the country. Some treks are quite enjoyable and some are quite difficult and full of adventure.

5. Sarahan Wangtu Trek: We can trek from Sarahan to Wangtu with great enthusiasm and spirit of dedicated trekker. It is one of the most lively and beautiful trekking routes in the world. The trekking routes passes through the villages Sungra and Nechar where a few ancient temples welcome us in peace and serenity. There are some rest houses which dates back to 1890. We can enjoy some days here.

(*a*) At first day we can leave Sarahan to Chora. This is a sixteen km. pleasant north east to Hindustan-Tibet road. The path leads to through a beautiful forests of pine, horse-chestnut, oak and rhododendron. The trail is fairly level to start with but after a km it descends and crosses two streams, it continues down gently to the Chora forest rest house. An ancient temple of Hirma Devi is located at 300 metres below the rest house.

(*b*) On second day we can approach to Tranda which is 8 km from Chora.

(*c*) On third day, we can leave for Paunda which is 10 km from Tranda.

(*d*) On fourth day, we can proceed on to Nechar which is 12 km from Paunda.

(*e*) On fifth day we can advance to Wangtu through Nechar which is 5 km from Nechar. Wangtu (31°32¢N, 78°01E) is on Hindustan Tibet road and from there we can catch a bus direct for Shimla or we can return back to Sarahan for more holidaying and enjoy camp life in the wilderness.

We can advance in the area of tourism management by developing human resources, creating more employment opportunities and spreading wealth to rural areas where poverty and unemployment are rife. The high prioyity should be given to basic principles of eco-tourism, ensuring compatibility with ecological sensitivity and extending benefits to surrounding communities where it is possible. The eco-tourism, wildlife and nature conservation can gain a new momentum in the management and modernisation of tourism activities just to make it more interesting and affordable.

6. Adventure Sports : Rampur Bushahar and Sarahan have a very beautiful background for adventure sports and eco-tourism activities. These should be encouraged with better efforts and inspirations.

15

The Wild Birds of Sarahan

Mountains are the greatest recreation in the world. These are sacred destinations to enjoy life. To spend long time holidays the mountains are best recreation points for the lovers of nature. They are the symbols of courage, beauty and joy. In the Hindu scriptures, the Himalaya is the incarnation of Lord Shiva and Lord Vishnu. The high mountain peaks, flowering pastures, deep narrow valleys, serpentine rivers and gorges remain full of nature's prestine beauty and inspires us in many ways. Sarahan is a beautiful place in Rampur Bushahar where the nature lovers, explorers, trekkers and tourists from far and near come to enjoy life admidst the vast expanded forests.

The place is considered among the world's most beautiful natural and relaxation point during the summer months. Sarahan is surrounded by most beautiful mountains peaks, wildlands and valleys and can be enjoyed in every season. The winter months are bitter cold and the summer days are more pleasant. The valleys remain warm in winter as well as summer.

Location: Sarahan is situated over a hill-rock at the height of 9500′. It is 80 kilometer from Rampur Bushahar and is considered the summer capital of Rampur Bushahar. Rampur Bushahar is 176 kilometers from Shimla. The Rampur is the most ancient traditional city situated on the bank of river Satluj. Satluj is a calm, deep and devastating river which during the rainy season creates a havoc to the people living near its banks. The road upto Sarahan is quite comfortable and full of enjoyment. The serpentine roads, lush green valleys, gushing pure water streams and beautiful forest patches not only recreate to human mind but provide a lot of enjoyment also for holiday makers during summer as well as winter. Tourism in winter days is also quite high because of snow fall and to enjoy adventure sports like skiing, skatting and ideal camp life amidst the nature. Religious tourism and family tourism is high during pleasant summer days.

Sarahan: Nature's Peaceful Paradise: Sarahan is nature's peaceful paradise and the "Queen of Spring". This is the most pleasant tourist place to enjoy holidays during spring as well as winter. Many stories are related to Sarahan from the very beginning of Mahabharata period. This is the place where the powerful warrior Bheema Sena (Bheema of Mahabharata) took the form of a beautiful woman to allure Lord Vishnu. As a result a huge temple from Mahabharata period came into existence in this place. The temple is known as Maa Bheemakali Temple with most ancient idols in the area. The religious tourists and pilgrims from far and near come to visit the temple to have the "Darshan" of Mother Bheemakali the Great Goddess of the people of Rampur Bushahar. Some villages in this belt are most ancient, said to be from Mahabharata period and are known for their great cultural heritage from the ancient time.

Shrikhand Mahadev: Here, a natural rock is formed into a large Shivalinga and is known as Shrikhand Mahadev. The mountain is expanded upto the height of 18000 and is standing just opposite Sarahan. Sarahan and Shrikhand Mahadev are the most enjoyable destinations for trekking expeditions during summer as well as winter months. During snowfall, Sarahan is fully covered with the white silver carpet of snow which creates more enchanting view. The slopes in Sarahan and surrounding forests are used for skiing and skatting during the snowfall.

When the temperature falls down to minus degree centigrades, the river and streams freeze into snow. The wind remains harsh and violent during the whole winter and it is bitter cold after snow fall.

The winter is harsh and summer is pleasant during the months of summer. The spring comes with youthful approach and the flora of the whole region turns into a new growing look in the environment. The trees, plants, bushes, herbs and wild vegetables grow with new buds and leaves. The wild flowers and aromatic plants provide a kind of sweet fragrance into the environment and make it the most pleasant place for trekking, exploration and bird watching. Sarahan is internationally known for their rich and varied bird life. The famous birds of the Western Himalayas are found here into the deodar forests and open wild lands. The forests are spread upto 14000′. Among most beautiful birds are Monal Pheasant, Jaju Rana, Western Himalayan snow cock, western Himalayan Tragopan, Kocklash, Khalij Pheasant, Palash, Ratnal, teetar and bater all are found in the valleys of the high mountain pastures. During heavy snow fall they come to the lower foothills and warm valleys.

The Wild Bird Sanctuary: Sarahan represents the most suitable eco-system of the Western Himalayan mountains. It has all the necessary elements of Western Himalayan eco-system as a result Western Himalayan Bird Sanctuary is established here. The experts of the mountain flora and fauna explain that the summer as well as winter climate are the most suitable for the flora and fauna of Sarahan. That's why the wild bird sanctuary in Saharan is the most popular one in the world. There are more than 144 wild mountain birds in the cages of wild bird sanctuary. The avifauna lovers and bird watchers have a great fascination for these birds. To observe the rare birds of Western Himalayas is not only recreating but highly exciting to the mind. The birds like Monal—Lophorus impejanus, Western Himalayan Tragopan, Red snow cock, Jaju Rana and Khalij Pheasants are the most amazing birds of the Western Himalayas.

We can observe several mountain peaks, pasturelands, forests and fresh water streams when we approach at the Sarahan mountain top. The view point is most enchanting and creates nature's beautiful sites. The view points are enjoyed by the regular pilgrims, tourists and local trekkers.

The view from Sarahan playground creates a marvellous scene of the local mountain peaks, waterfalls, dense forests and steep rocks. Sarahan airport also presents a beautiful view and prepares for a happy landing for the travellers and explorers coming from far and near.

The tourists who come to visit Sarahan wild bird sactuary and Maa Bheemakali temple were from Australia, Newzealand, Japan, Canada, USA and Germany. Most of the foreign tourists who visited this place liked it in many ways. For example the place is a best asset in nature watching and exploration activities. All the rare birds of the Western Himalayas are found in the wildlife sanctuary of Sarahan. The place has become an ideal bird watching centre in the Himachal Pradesh.

Besides these rare birds, the other local birds are also found in the valleys and ravines of Sarahan. Among these birds are teetar, bater, chakore, wild fowl, black wild fowls and exact red wild fowls in the dense forests and hedges.

The singing birds like koel, kafoo, peeyu, skylark, red finch and black finch are found in the bushes and open pastures of valleys and slopes. The wild pigeons, turtle dove and Dom crow are visible in the forests.

The place is an excellent location for bird studies and bird watching activities. The small bushes, berries and fruit trees are quite safe in this area which are the main habitats and hiding places for the small birds. The most beautiful colour birds and singing birds are found in the small fruit bushes in the valleys which remain warm during winter winds. The summer days are full of pleasure and enjoyment as a result we can have a camplife near the valleys and pasture slopes where the harsh cold winds do not easily penetrate.

The birds also come into the open pastures from the dark bushes to enjoy the sun during winter and this is the proper time when we can observe them from very near. With the help of a telescope, we can watch the birds without any disturbance and can enjoy the game with our best. The birds have three types of habitation. The small birds always like to remain in warm valleys. The great pheasant birds like to live in the open pastures and forests near the peaks. The normal size birds like to inhabit in the middle heights of the mountains as they remain dark and dense with trees and bushes. Also an ideal place for hiding and nesting. The middle heights are also important for such birds as they can have a watch on the enemies from all around which are coming to search or destroy their nests. The enemies include, jackals, giant squirrel, snakes, small prey birds and the eagles (local small mountain eagles who nest amidst high rocks and old tree cavities).

Besides bird watching, we can proceed on to nature watching activities in the Sarahan mountain peaks and valleys.

The ideal nature watching spots are lush green forests, dark bushes, dangerous steep rocks, amazing rock pieces standing amidst the river water. The gushing fresh water streams, pleasant river banks, distant forest patches and sparkling waterfalls are a prized testimony for all of us.

From Sarahan Hotel Complex we can view the beautiful peaks of Srikhand Mahadev, surrounding mountains, orchards, forests, villages and the temples glowing with a bright day sun.

Exploration Activities: Sarahan is a heaven for exploration and trekking activities. We can start our expeditions direct from Rampur Bushahar toward Sarahan either through river banks or through the bus route or by on foot. Such efforts are very useful and pleasant to observe the valleys and see the nature from a very close look. It proves precisely enjoyable and full of delight. Anything which we do ourselves practically develops confidence and self reliance in us. These exploration activities in many ways are a great reward for us in life. We should happily accept the challenges and make them successful through our great efforts. If a person is fully determined to fulfil the assigned task the half work is done immediately. Now it is quite clear that we should proceed on with our main goal and should overcome the challenges with full determination.

Trekking, exploration and mountaineering are the best mountain sports full of recreation. Some other sports of snow are also useful and adventurous. We should do our best to enjoy these great challenges of our life.

The Ideal Camp Life: There are so many fascinating places for great human recreation. These places are of natural importance and useful for ideal camp life. First of all during summer or spring the Satluj Banks are best location as they remain warm, pleasant and full of wild flowers. It becomes more enjoyable to take tea, coffee and refreshment with the company of friends. When we are in groups we generally talk about national and international affairs and analyse the international reports and despatches by various newspaper correspondents. This becomes an ideal debate and we all participate to give our decision and impartial opinion on the various issues related to the problems of a particular country.

When we are trekking from one place to another the tea or coffee becomes quite tasteful in the colder places in the mountains. As a result we drink at least twelve cup of tea or coffee in a day. This provides extra-energy and creates enthusiasm to get ahead. It is certain that to take more tea or coffee is not harmful when you are continuously working hard or trekking from one place to another. It gives extra enjoyment of life and the taste of the tea becomes more sweet and full of extra energy. The trekker refreshes himself and remains in high spirit for his further expeditions. This has provided us a very nice experience of trekking and camping in the wild of Himachal Pradesh. For the best camp life, the slopy protective pastures, strong rock-caves, plain land between two hillocks which completely blocks the external winds and waves coming towards the tents. The camp can also be organised in the open forest land which is far from violent animals like leopards, mountain tigers, bears, wild foxes and snakes. Sarahan forest land is also among the most suitable places for ideal camp sites and relaxation points.

The Fauna and Flora: The heavenly land of Sarahan is rich in fauna and flora. The wild animals and plants found in the range of Western Himalayan Ecosystem are very much found here. Particularly, all the varieties of mountain flowers and aromatic plants are found within the range of Sarahan and Rampur Bushahar.

The Fauna: This is related to wild life of the Western Himalayas. The height of Sarahan mountain peak is more than 11,000′ and there is heavy snowfall during the winter. The mountain peaks of Sarahan are covered with 6-7′ snow. Sometime, there is snowfall three or four times and the record of snow fall goes up to 12′. During this snowfall, all the rare birds and wild animals are visible in the snow landscape of Sarahan. For example mountain deers, Ghoral, fox, bears, tigers, rabits and other important mammals are spotted moving in search of food in the snow covered forests of the surrounding mountains. The wild goats or ghoral reside over the dangerous rocks which are steep and slippery. No other animal can pass through these rocks. In this way these animals remain safe from the attack of violent animals.

The wild animals and birds come to the warm valleys and live there for some days unless the violent winds and snowfall stops the wild birds like Monal, Jaju Rana, Western Himalayan Tragopan, Red snow cock, Ratnal, Palash, Khalij Pheasant, Kocklash, Teetar, Bater and Chakore come to the valleys and inhabit inside the warm bushes or rock cavities. During snowfall and bitter cold they come to the foothills, valleys and near the river banks as these spots remain comparatively warmer rather than the upper hill areas.

The Flora: Sarahan is a paradise for wild vegetables, plants and trees. During the summer days, the whole mountain region is aglow with new buds, vegetations, wild flowers and aromatic plants. There are various species of ferns, moss, orchids, lily and insectivorous plants. Riccia and Marcantia can be seen near water streams, moisturous places or those places from where the water leaks from the rocks. The alpine moss is found over the moisturous rocks, dark wet valleys, and near slopy pastures. The alpine moss is long in height, very thin and the capsules are needle like. It is found at the height upto 13,000′.

The Fern: There are six types of ferns in Sarahan. The fern species varies from 6 inches to six feet height. They are a big recreation to human life.

1. One is edible fern and used in vegetables. This fern is known as "Lingad" in Himachali language and linguda in Garhwali language.
2. The most exciting thing is the orchid—The terrestrial orchids are found in the forests and mountains upto the height of 11,000.
3. The Himalayan Lily's flowering plants have been observed in this area by the botanists and nature explorers. Besides this, there are several varieties of wild flowers and alpine plants in the wilderness of Sarahan which are more exciting and beautiful to observe.

The Orchids: There are several species of common terrestrial orchids with yellow flowers and an opaque tubers with them. (The number of tubers, in some plants is upto 10). But there is only one main tuber with main plant and the other tubers are formed in various small roots. (Location of such orchids is Sarahan forest land, Jubbal-Kupped forests, Tumroo Peak-Khara Pather in Jubbal, Chanshal Valley near Larot village, Talra forests in Tharoch, Ishon in Pyuntra valley, Moralu Pasture in Bairog, Tharoch and fascinating Deiya forests. The forests of Chaupal tehsil are known for the best orchid species. Some examples are of Lady's Slipper orchids, with dark red, golden, yellow flowers, and the common terrestrial orchids with light-green-yellow flowers. There are at least more than 20 species of terrestrial orchids found in the area.

Some of the orchids are the best terrestrial species and are aromatic in nature with immense medicinal values. A nursery of such invaluable species can be cultivated inside the forest lands to use them for the medicinal purpose at the commercial scale. In such forest nursery the species are propagated in the nature and are left free to grow. After their growth, they can be used for the commercial use and some of them can be left in the nature to grow again. Such species of the orchids can be planted all over the moisturous parts of the mountains so that they may grow again and again.

The Ferns: The ferns found here are of seven types:

1. Dragon fern
2. Spider fern
3. Poisonous fern (Bishlingad)
4. Edible fern (lingad)
5. Ornamental fern
6. Single leef ferns
7. Mini ferns which grow near the moss and other miniplants in the shades and moisturous areas.

Spider fern is found in the moisturous parts of Sarahan. It's leaves are just like spider's web. It is found in upper and middle heights. The Dragon fern is a rough bush of ferns found in the valleys. It is quite hard and its growth reaches upto six feets. The other ferns are common at the pastures and valleys at the lower heights. One red varieties of fern which is poisonous is found at the 9000–11000′ heights.

The Moss: The moss found in the mountains is of three types:

1. The moss at lower valleys with a large capsules and dwarf plant.
2. The moss with a normal capsules and normal plant at middle height.
3. The moss at upper heights needle like plant and needle like capsules.

The Scenic Valley of Narkanda: Narkanda is a most enjoyable tourist place during summer as well as winter. Particularly for summer, it is a most pleasant place for trekking and camp life. It is some 60 km from Rampur Bushahar and 50 km from Theog. It has the most dense forests in the area with cool breeze caressing us in the months of summer. The full bloom pastures of wild flowers welcome us with sweet fragrance into the air.

Narkanda is situated at the height of 9,500. It is among the most beautiful natural sites to visit and relax into the lap of mother nature. The valley from Narkanda creates most magnificent panoramic views during summer as well as winter. It is most auspicious to visit Narkanda from May to August. It has got its natural charm, grandeure and magnificence from its scenic mountains and valleys. During summer and winter the valleys are covered with misty environment.

Narkanda is the main trekking point from where we can proceed on towards four directions. But we have to chose one direction at a time while trekking through the mountains slopes and valleys. It becomes more enjoyable and enchanting trekking through ancient routes which pass through the forests and mountains. When we view Narkanda Valley from the mountains top it turns into a real heaven to watch over.

Jalori Pass: From Narkanda we can proceed towards Jalori Pass. Jalori Pass is an ideal place for trekking and night camping. At Jalori slopes we can have a better camp sites with safe surrounding. It is a wonderful place to trek and relax into the lap of mother nature.

This trek is extremely enjoyable and easy, with beautiful valleys and landscapes in Himachal Pradesh.

The lush green forests, pastures with carpet grass with rich flora and fauna, sparkling streams and magnificent snowclad mountains in winter all around make this trek an unforgettable experience of life.

If we want to enjoy the beauty and peace of Narkanda we have to reach here three days in advance to explore the new possibilities of adventure sports. There are some excellent nature watching sites for the physical and mental recreations. From here we can encourage several outdoor activities.

16

Wilderness and Bio-diversity

What is Bio-diversity?

The bio-diversity is a natural wealth of life over this earth. This includes micro-organisms, insects, plants and animals. The plants and animals are a part of the bio-diversity. Also, the genes they contain and the eco-system they help to buildup in the living environment. The existing form of bio-diversity we see today is the result of four billion years of evolution of life over this earth. Bio-diversity conservation helps in creating a thriving eco-system over this earth. Hence, we should continue our efforts for the protection of bio-diversity and nature conservation activities.

Whenever we destroy nature, we destroy bio-diversity. Although our lives are dependent on it. Bio-diversity provides eco-system stability, biological production (everythings we eat, hence economic stability, medicinal herbs, housing material (wood), clothing and fuel.

Bio-diversity is also the basis of many religions, cultures and aesthetic values.

In modern time, the worst effected part of this earth is the fragile mountain environment and the fresh water eco-systems. The expansion of the human population has resulted into the loss of bio-diversity. Almost all human activities sooner or later effect a fresh water eco-systems *i.e.,* a brook, river, pond or lake. This results into the habitat destruction, air precipitation and water pollution.

Besides this, the mountain environment is the most fragile one and is easily destroyed by felling of woods, forest fire, devastating rain and by over grazing by the cattles of Gujjars. The Gujjars are the forest dwellers which cause much more damage to the mountain forests. Talra wilderness and other mountain pastures are worst effected by them.

The worst thing is that they are not literate at all. They do not understand values of trees and plants. There is a regular wood felling by them for making the house (Deras) in the wild. The precious cancer medicinal tree of Taxus Buccata is found here. Besides this, there are atleast ten species of terrestrial orchids with medicinal values. The wilderness is the nursery of 110 wild flowering plants. There are several wild animals and rare birds. For our projects we have taken *Talra Wilderness and Wild life Sanctuary in the Himachal Pradesh.*

The reasons of taking Talra Wilderness for our project study.

1. It is important wild life sanctuary with rare plants and trees. There are 110 flowering herbs, medicinal plants in this wilderness.
2. The world's most important terrestrial orchids, about ten species are found in this mountain. The best and largest Lady's slipper orchid is found in this height of 9000'. Taxus buccata, the anti-cancer plant is found in this mountain.
3. The mountain is the most beautiful place for visitors, trekkers, explorers and researchers. It is widely known for its rich eco-tourism prospects.
4. The maximum damage to this high mountain wilderness is done by the Gujjars illegal felling of several trees for the purpose of their "Deras". Their cattle also create a lot of damage to the nature by rupturing the pastures, valleys and trekking routes. (2) The local tribals and villagers also damage the forests in various ways. (3) The goat and sheep grazers also damage the nature by over grazing. (4) They pollute fresh water sources.

The Initiation: First of all we travelled village to village in Tharoch area and taught the people about "what is wilderness and what is bio-diversity!" The village people liked our programme to protect a wilderness like "the Moonlit Mountains of Talra". It was nice to work amidst the villagers. Talra is a beautiful wildlife sanctuary and deserves to be protected from the external encroachment.

Our next programme was in the swamp forests of Dehradun

where the PTS groups joined us with great inspiration to protect the swamp forests of Chidderwala. The people openly came forward to protect the orchid forests of Dehradun (Chidderwala Forest Range-swamp area) and protected two important orchid species of this area (1) Vanda Cristata (2) Obenoria. Both of the species of orchid are almost endangered in the swamp forests because of regular encroachment of land and forests by the forest mafias, local dwellers and tribals. We have completed a decade of our mass awareness campaign and orchid conservation workshops in more than 200 schools and colleges in the area with the co-operation of Parents, Teachers and Volunteers. Established International Orchid Clubs in some villages and towns of Uttaranchal.

Mass Awareness Campaign Through Schools and Colleges: The school children are the best communicators in the environment awareness and nature conservation activities. On several occasions, we organised parents teachers and students meetings to start a mass awareness campaign from the schools and colleges in Himachal Pradesh and in Uttaranchal Hills. In this way, we were quite successful in organising workshops on medicinal herbs and ornamental plants and their conservation near the villages, schools and colleges. The students were told about their benefits to human being as a result many students, parents and teachers followed us and have established Environment Clubs, Nature Conservation Clubs, The Wild Fern Clubs, The Oak Tree Clubs, The Honey Bird Club, The Asian Elephant Club. The Swamp Forests Clubs, The Orchid Clubs and Wild Palnt Study Clubs in their houses with the support of highly qualified parents. This mass awareness project by International Institute of Mountain Studies and Research was the most successful project by now.

The nature conservation activities, wilderness management and location of Important Plant Areas (IPA) were most inspiring and enjoyable activities among PTA and volunteers.

The school children were the most powerful communicators of our campaigns in the hills.

It has become an interesting hobby among the students to schools and colleges.

IPA, MPZ, Wildreness: Locating Important Plant Areas (IPA) in famous alpine pastures, Chanshal valley is an Important Medicinal Plant Zone and eco-tourism destination for the trekkers and adventure lovers. The wild herbsare found at the height of 14000, Jubbal-Kupped 13000 and Turmroo mountain 9500 in Himachal Pradesh (Khara Pather 1994-1995.) Again, from January to August 1997, we located 110 ethnobotanical medicinal plants, fruits and wild flowers. We had a team of experts to locate medicinal plants, fruits and wild flowers.

Mass Support for Conservation Activities: For the first time in the history of nature conservation, a large number the village women of Himachal came out openly from their houses to co-operate with us in locating medicinal plants in the local forests, wilderness and pastures in Tharoch area. In Deharadun, Chidderwala, Saung river banks swamp area and Kansher Forest Range, we had located many outstanding species of medicinal plants, and prepared medicinal powder from them. Most of them were traditional medicines used by local villagers and tribals. In Toya River, Swamp area, Shoni shot, Shishuwa nala, Nababwala plot and Barkot Wilderness, Dehradun, we had located may IPA (Important Plant Areas and wildlands) in Dehradun Chidderwala region.

"Wilderness Management and Sustaining Harvest of Medicinal Plants": Wilderness management and non-timber products were very interesting subjects for the local villagers who knew about the sustaining harvest of non-forest products and their benefits for the people. This was done in Srikot, Baheli, Simtoli, and Daaligaad area during 1996-97. The Baheli and Daaligaad Wilderness, mountain vegetation at Gaamaath, medicinal plants of Ghoraa Dhungee Pasture land and other Important Plant Areas were located in the same region and the spots were marked for the future studies and collection of medicinal plants as sample from the wild.

The main emphasis was given on nature conservation in the villages and school surroundings. The students participated in such activities.

International Conservation Clubs: The parents and teachers established three International Nature Conservation clubs in Bubakhal, Srikot and Simtoli in Pauri Garhwal for monitoring the local conservation activities as these three areas are under the Important Plant Zones. The main emphasis was given on medicinal and wild vegetable food plants and their utilization at the local and commercial scale. Sustainable harvesting of medicinal plants and wild vegetables for food in the gardens as well as forest areas in the hill region were the main topics of study. In some areas, it was found that the whole village population can survive on wild vegetables the year round. We have marked the areas of such food vegetables. For example Simtoli, Baheli, Ginthali (PAURI) and Chidderwala in Dehradun. were located prominently.

Sustainable Harvesting of Swamp Forests: The swamp forests are the fresh water mangroves full of botanical wealth and are quite useful to the local people. First of all, we selected a ten kilometers area of swamp forest for our conservation studies. The area is quite rich in aquatic edible plants, medicinal herbs and numerous useful vegetable foods for the local people inhabiting and surrounding it. Our main aim was to conserve the area thoroughly and use it to its maximum for the purpose of wild foods, fruits, and vegetables useful to the local population. It is estimated that more than 60,000 people surrounding the swamp area and 1.5 lakh people along the Saung river in Dehradun are regularly using fruits, vegetables and medicinal plants for their foods. We did five things for the conservation and the survival of "Swamp Forest land" in Chidderwala.

(1) To stop all the illegal felling and anti forest activities in the area within ten kilometers

(2) It was declared protected zone and 20 Nature Conservation Clubs were established by International Institute of Mountain Studies And Research and protecting it regularly.

(3) The village people were taught about sustainable harvesting of swamp vegetables, medicinal plants, fishes and wild fruits and beries!

(4) Conservation and management of Swamps Areas is a people's mass awareness campaign for the protection of swamp forests.

(5) The swamps are a fresh water mangroves and the water is neat and clean almost drinkable and the people were taught not to pollute it and should try their best to protect it and keep it always clean and fresh. They can use vegetables but they have no right to pollute it.

The swamp forests have rich and amazing bio-diversity. It has a marvellous wealth of wild plants.

Protecting the Biodeversity of Swamp Forests of Dehradun: At least seven species of wild vegetable foods, 10 species of wild fruits, five species of wild beries are found in the swamps. In the ten kilometer areas, 1.5 lakh people are using the swamp food vegetables and herbal medicines. The non-forest products are used regularly by the tribal people. The swamps are free from pollution and encroachment now. The "Shishua", "Linguda", "Wild Pindalu" and saunf plants are an ideal food vegetables. The wild Saunf plants and peppermint, both the aromatic and medicinal plants have great importance for the villagers. They get five types of vegetable foods for the year round and even when the vegetable season is gone, the Swamp Forest is a boon for them! The people have understood the true meaning of nature conservation and sustainable harvesting of wild fruits and vegetables in the Swamp forests. This has become more meaningful and enjoyable for the local villagers and tribals inhabiting the surrounding of swamp area. Various tribal and non-tribal communities use the vegetables from swamp forests and almost survive on swamp vegetables in every season. The Bogsha tribals are the original dwellers of swamp forests and they have unique cultural traditions. We all writers, scholars and volunteers are protecting this amazing wetland of Chidderwala. It is also providing us great delight to preserve their cultural heritage, folk songs ancient tradition and social and religious activities.

Our exploration spirit encourages for other future activities. Self exploration and travelling is the best way to reach to the close of nature. This provides us new experience, ideas and training for nature conservation and outdoor education.

Narkanda and Hatoo Peak: We took complete rest after arriving at Narkanda and proceed on the next day. Private lodges and guest houses are available at the minimal charges. For this purpose one should have proper work schedule and successful planning for the future activities in trekking and exploration. The natural beauty of Hatoo Peak and Narkanda valley impresses us the most. The place is quite beautiful for adventure sports activities.

The future strategy to explore the nature should be clear in your mind.

The next day we can approach to famous peak Hatoo at 11,000 and can return back in the evening to our base camp at Narkanda. We can face here Goddess Hatoo, the most ancient Goddess in the area. At Hatoo, we can have an ideal camp life. Famous politician Raja Virbhandra Singh and other devotees come here every year to offer Puja ceremony to mother Goddess Hatoo during summer.

On third day, we should leave Narkanda early in the morning after breakfast. We reach Kharag with surface transport, take lunch enroute. We reach Kharag in the evening. We are tired and half hearted with our day by day journey. At Kharag we can organise over night camp at 8500′.

On the fourth day, we would like to approach to a beautiful lake via Jalori Pass at the height of 10,280 and return back to the camp the same day. This becomes an unforgettable journey with the sweet and sour experiences of trekking difficulties in Jalori pass.

It becomes quite a memorable experience if the company is good and adventure spirit continues. We can spend time with lively innovative outdoor activities.

On the 5th day, we proceed on to Raghuvir Singh Fort (The famous ancient fort of a brave ruler) at 11,000 and after exploring the area we return back to the camp.

On Sixth day, We leave the Kharag Camp and after break fast we reach to Narkanda in the evening. We have overnight stay at Narkanda and slept well in the night after dinner. It was a memorable experience of life enjoying a peaceful environment in the mountains and dense forests.

On Seventh day, we depart after breakfast and arrive back to their respective destinations abreast with very sweet memories and experiences of life and the scenic mountains of Himachal Pradesh.

The life in Narkanda can be enjoyed with its fullest if we have good company of friends and we are free from external worries. We should be free and free and should enjoy nature's gifts with its every encounter of trekking life.

May-June, August-September are the best months to enjoy trekking exploring and ideal camplife. Narkanda is bitter cold during snowfall and is an ideal place for snow landscape studies. It is quite well known place for skiing, skating, horse riding, hang gliding, para gliding and night life camping amidst the dense forests.

There is a peculiar ecology of wilderness and wild lands. A though study and research work is necessary for the extensive knowledge of their bio-diversity.

The mammals, replites, monkeys, bird fauna, butterflies, beetles, firebeetles and other insects are found in the wilderness. They have a world of natural co-existence in the nature and support each other's survival.

In this way the eco-system of the wilderness should be preserved for a longer period. The eco-system should not perish at all as it supports the life supporting system of all animals including human beings.

The eco-system and bio-diversity should be protected by all positive means as they are an important part of the ecology of this earth.

17

The Wilderness and Wild Fire

The wilderness and the forests have a thriving bio-diversity. These are a heaven to enjoy exploration activities. The world citizen should do their best to protect them for the future generation.

Unfotunately, a large part of such natural lands over this earth is destroyed by wild fire every year. The great wilderness of Amazonia in Brazil, Oak forests o Greece, dry forests of California, Florida and Wisconsin catch fire every year and a large part of forest is destroyed in the fire. There is a big loss of wild life, trees and plants species. In India, several large forests have been destroyed in the forest fires. Any way, we should control this devastating fire through our disaster management efforts. This is a call of the hour! The expanded wildlands are the natural form of wilderness. Such amazing wild lands are a great source of enjoyment for the lovers of nature. For example amazing British Columbia (Canada) Rajaji National Park (India) and South Africa's, Kruger National Park are among the best wildlands in the world. Such places are a great source of eco-tourism activities in the world.

Wild fire quickly spreads in our forests and wilderness. The nature lovers and aware citizens and trekkers should extinguish it with their best efforts. It becomes quite difficult to control it when it spreads in four directions and the wild winds make it easy to turn into a ravaging interno. Most of our plant, trees and wild animals vanish away during the forest fire. In India, particularly, pine, deodar and oak forests catch fire immediately because of their quick burning quality. The pine and deodar leaves are full of oil glands which burns quickly.

Dangers of Wild fire

Forest fire cause the worst destruction of the forests and wildlands which result into the loss of bio-diversity. This also hampers the plans of forests and wildland management in a big way. We have lost some species of wild plants and trees in the hill areas of Himachal, Uttaranchal and North - Eastern India. It should be extinguished and controlled by every possible means.

The moisturous forests and moisture loving plants are safe from such devastating fires but some time, the growth of trees and plants is also destroyed by the raging inferno.

The worst sufferers are pine and kail forests as their leaves are highly inflamable. The cedar trees are also harmed in this array but some of them remain safe because of moisture.

During summer days, there are several incidents of forest fire. In "Himachal and Uttaranchal" both the state have enough forest land in the country in camparison to other states. Total forest area in Himachal is 22 percent and total forest area in Utteranchal remains upto 45-48%. Uttaranchal is the only state in the country to have largest forest cover.

The incidents of forest fires in Himachal and Uttaranchal are common and every year during summer a large number of fauna and flora is destroyed from the forests.

There are some good reasons for that :

(1) We have a good well organised mass awareness movement in Uttaranchal for the past 30 years.

(2) Most of the NGOS are supporting conservation and reforestation activities. The forests and wilderness remain safe because of intelligent trekkers and explorers. The citizens report regularty to forest officers on any mishappening.

(3) Some citizens do not use forest wood at all.

(4) We have given good coverage to press regarding the felling, landslide, earthquake, floods in the river, conservation of orchid forests of Dehradun, the high mountain wilderness in India, Wilderness management and eco-tourism activities are best organised in our

country. Very few forests were fell down by corporation and forest mafias and because of social awareness, felling speed has slowed down since then. But secretly and silently the wood smuggling is going on in the adjoining areas of forests.

(5) The people are growing extra fuel and fodder woods into their fields and woodlands for their own use. The grown up wood is sold to paper mills. Sometime the wood is collected from the workers and contractors of the paper mills. In some parts of the country the wood smuggling is continue.

Three adjoining areas of forests are damaged in the roaring fire.

There are three reasons to cause forest fire.

(1) By the igrorant citizens
(2) Deliberate fire by grazers, forests mafias.
(3) By forest fire: self generated fire from the friction of old trees.

Sometimes it becomes quite impossible to control forests fire as it spreads quickly in multiple directions with the movement of air. There are reports that incalculable damage has been done to the forests by the forest fire in the past. The trees are burnt to death by fires and those survived are completely charred and disfigured. The charred plants have no possibity to grow again.

The pine and kail forests are more susceptible to Spruce and Silver fir but is very dangerous in young deodar plantations. Chil fir is hardly acceptable in very young age. But such growth is partially damaged by the forest fire.

The immense damage was caused by the forest fire of 1920-21, 1930-31, 1939-40, 1945-48, 1952-53, 1969-70 and 1971-72 in which a fully grown forest crop was burnt into a large scale. In 1998, there were incidents of forest fire in Himachal and Uttaranchall hill districts where one third of the forests were burnt down because of raging inferno.

In some incidents, the forest fire may be accidental or deliberate, but in most cases it was found that it was deliberately played upon trick by some anti social elements.

Careless stubble burning in the punwis, smoking and careless handling of torchwood are the main cause of accidental fires. Here, the precaution should be maintained during the forest fire in the hills.

Forest fires caused by natural happenings such as lightening or rolling of stones or fricition between dry bamboos -such cases were found very rare. It is seen that the villagers or the unscrupulous elements set the forest on fire deliberately during the dry months of April to December.

The extent to damage caused by fires varies with condition and composition of the crop, aspect undergrowth, presence of felling - refuse and season of occurrence.

Damage is less in the properly thinned and heavily grazed stands- provided these are kept clean of the felling refuse.

In the year of 1998 and 1999, there was wild fire in the forests of Himachal and Uttaranchal and almost destroyed everything in the devastating fire. In the above fire, several plants and tree species were completely wiped out, several insects, birds, animals and the habitats were destroyed away.

The herbs, wild flowering plants were burnt into the ashes. The young calves of deer, rabbits, shahees, wildfowls, the birds and their nests alongwith eggs were burnt down in the raging inferno of the forest.

There are several examples of forest fire in the forests of the world which has caused a heavy loss of bio-diversity as well as the wealth of local communities forest fire in Greece.

There were several instances of forest fire in Greece. There was a devastating fire in the year 2004 in which several cars, houses and forests were burnt. This fire was initiated by unknown elements. But the forest officers blamed the arsonists for this devastation.

The Inferno of Greece

In the year 1998, there was a devastating fire in the forests of Greece. These forests of Corck Oak are of international importance. In 1998 over 100,000 reported as having burnt. In the Peloponnese peninsula the Taygetos forest, Greece' richest forest in terms of bio-diversity, burnt for several days. It has more than 160 endemic plants species (of which 21 are exclusive to the forest itself) and 36 rare or endangered animal species.

Aristotelis Papageorgiou, WWF Greece forest officer blamed the arsonists wanting to clear land for settlement and development.

Barkot Range, Dehradun, India: In the year 2006, there was a raging inferno in the forests of Toya-Barkot Range, Dehradun. This was the handi-work of some arsonists in the area. This was jointly extinguished with the efforts of forest Chauki Incharge, Chiderwala and Barkot Range Officers with immediate effect. The forest officers, Range Officers, Beat Officers and forest guards and helpers had shown immense courage to extinguish the fire on time. Range officers Ajeet Singh, Rawat, Rajendra Singh Negi, Beat Officer Ramesh Singh Rawat, Forest Guard Devendra Bisht with their assistants immediately started their efforts to control the fire from four directions. There are some grave incidents of forest fire in Rajaji National Park and Barkot Range Dehradun but the fire is controlled with immediate effect by the efforts of officers and forest guards.

It is also worth to mention here that chief conservator (wild life) Shreekant Chandola, DFO, Ranjan Mishra and other officers working in Dehradun have done their best to protect the pristine forests and wildlife of Uttaranchal state. They have come forward when ever we required their co-operation. There is more awareness and sensitivity and forests of our country are more well protected and safe now. We should continue to protect our wild lans and forests with our best efforts. This is the need of the hour.

The local volunteers, villagers and NGOs working on nature conservation are quite sensitive now.

18

Mountain Resorts and Eco-Tourism

There are some beautiful mountain resorts in Himachal, Uttaranchal, Sikkim and other states known for their abound natural beauty. The main aim of such resorts is to encourage nature lovers, health loving tourists, honeymoon goers, nature watchers and bird lovers.

The high budget tourists, businessmen, company executives, administrators, managers and planners come to attend business meetings and successful planning in the mountain resorts. These resorts have been popular among VIPS, and executives for long business meetings and conferences and have proved peaceful destinations among the foreigners staying here for the longer period.

Mountaineers, trekkers and lovers of snow sports visit such resorts for peace and happiness.

The resorts in the interiors of UK, Ireland, Spain, France, Greece Mexico, Brazil, India, Srilanka, Nepal, Japan, Philippines, South Africa and other countries with abound natural beauty doing a lot of good business. Such resorts have become the soul of nature tourism.

At present in our country, there are 2500 tourist resorts, nature resorts, health resorts, hotel resorts, adventure resorts and mountain beauty resorts. These are selected for their natural beauty, excellence and popularity among the visitors. There is large number of actual resorts in the country which are known for their multipurpose aim in various fields of life.

When a magnificent building is surrounded by a deodar forest, it becomes a known place for tourists and businessmen. Such places are known as Mountain Resorts as they are situated amidst the beautiful forests and green valleys in the mountains. At present day, these resorts have become the centres of eco-tourism activities where all sorts of tourists come and go. Such resorts in the mountains are turning into the great tourists destinations in modern. eco-tourism activities. The magnificent historical building of the by gone British era seem like a diamond studded necklace in the night while travelling through the Mall in Shimla, the capital of modern Himachal. Woodville Palace is a living paradise depicting the glory of the past and the present is rightly called the jewel of Shimla.

Shimla, once the summer capital of British India, situated at the 7000' above sea level, is the most enjoyable place for mountain tourism in modern days. The capital of Modern Himachal Pradesh it boasts of the grandeur of the glorious past and present. The snow clad mountain peaks in Western Himalayas almost rise up to 23,000' in attitude and have a great option for outdoor activities i.e. mountaineering, trekking and bird watching plus other adventure sports.

Shimla, the most impressive mountain city echoes the elegance and charm of an imperial past where Viceroys, Nobles and Princes maintained retreats to escape the scorching heat of plains in summer. A paradise for recreation and relaxation, Shimla, today offers to the visitors most enjoyable adventure sports like mountaineering, hang gliding, para gliding, riding, trekking, golfing, fishing, skating and skiing in winter. Bird watching is also a most enjoyable passtime activity in the valleys and forests during summer and winter days.

The British Heritage: Known for ancient British architecture, Shimla is considered the most comfortable place for enjoyment and holidaying. The old and new secretariats, Viceroy House, Wild flower Hall, Churches, bungalows of by gone Victorian age and other marvellous monuments of the past provide a warm welcome and delight to the visitors.

The surrounding of Shimla is well known for its outstanding scenic beauty. The wild flowers and important plant life zones impresses us along the road sides. It has a wonderful climate in summer and snowfall in winter. It is colder in the winter. A wealth of wild life options at Kufri, make it a unique eco-tourism destination in the Western Himalayan region.

The Famous Woodville Resorts: Among the most fascinating buildings of the past which boasts of its glory and charm, are all the beautiful buildings of British heritage. These are a sweet remembrence by now. The Woodvill Palace Resorts is a marvellous example of a unique palace-cum-Resorts in the modern days heritage tourism. Woodville Palace Resorts is a Princely retreat surrounded by wild flower bushes and pine and deodar forests. It is an amazing monument with a beautiful surrounding, popular for its absolute silence and unforgettable sunsets. With great peace and solitude, it is located in marvellous four acre land nestled with wild flower bushes, 150 pine and deodar trees. This beautiful mansion surpasses all Shimla residences in grandeur, dignity and serenity.

Scenic diversity is one of the most important attractions of Woodville resort. Resplendant with historic past, Woodville Palace was the abobe of the Commanders-in-Chief of the Imperial British Indian Army from 1860 to 1880. At that time the building was a fascimile of marvellous architecture and designing with stone and wood of Victorian age.

The famous writer Sir Edward Buck writes in his popular book 'Shimla: Past and Present', "The lawns of the Woodville were evidently the scene of many hard fought games of croquet in the eighteen sixties". It means Woodville Palace was a main place of conferences, games and recreation activities of British scholars and army commanders in 1860s.

With the pace of time the things started to change. In 1926, His Holiness Maharaja Sir Bhagat Singh of Gondal State in Western India purchased the property for his daughter Princess Leila. Princess Leila was a most beautiful and talented woman with great administrative qualities and Maharaja had a great affection for his daughter.

In 1938, the old Victorian building was demolished by her husband Raja Rana Sir Bhagat Chand, the most powerful ruler of Jubbal State. In those days, Jubbal State was one of the powerful Shimla Hill States of British India.

The present magnificent summer Palace was constructed during 1938 at a cost of Rs. five lakhs. Since the British rule, the Woodville Palace has been an abode of many famous world personalities, kings, queens, politicians, famous film directors, actors, actresses and VIPs of international repute. Jubbal State had an area of 288 square miles and was famous for its compact deodar forests. The Jubbal -Kupped wilderness is the most beautiful wilderness in the Jubbal Tehsil.

The world famous Kupped mountain is widely known for its enchanting beauty. Now it has become famous for sport activities like trekking picnicking and ideal location for shooting films. The Kupped and Tumroo mountains, according to the world famous botanists have all the species of wild flowers and Alpine plants. Some of them are quite useful for medicinal values.

Kupped and Tumroo are the beautiful pastures with Important Plant Areas. Both the mountains have important varieties of terrestrial orchids and vegetables. The maximum species of alpine plants, medicinal herbs, and wild flowers in the Western Himalayas which create an important plant life zone in the area are found here. This plant zone has become an immense centre of attraction for the botanists and trekkers of the world.

In modern days, Jubbal is widely known for its beautiful apple orchards and floriculture which provides its residents their main source of income. When the orchards are in full blossom, the Valley is particularly beautiful and during picking season the fragrance of fruits fills the air !

The Jubbal Royal family, belongs to the Rathore clan of Chandravanshee Rajputs who were renowned for their chivalry and bravery in the ancient time. Their origin can be traced back up to three hundred years with a well documented historical proof. In the past, Jubbal was the most powerful state in the Shimla Hills and still is known for its rich social, cultural and traditional values. Jubbal is famous for its religious values as it is a land of Gods and Goddesses. It has a well developed Himachali dialect, folklore, traditional dresses and is widely known for its rich cultural heritage.

Woodville Palace is related to the Princely family of Jubbal and it is important here to pin-point the facts about the family. Jai Peedhi Maa is the popular Goddess of Jubbal state and is worshipped with great faith and rejoice. The worship of Lord Mahasu and Jaagra festival is celebrated with great rejoice.

Raja Bhagat Chand, KCSI, one of the most enlightened rulers among Shimla Hill States, represented the Shimla Hill States in the Council of Princes from 1921-1924. He was made a CSI (Companion of the Star of India) in 1928 and KCSI (Knight Commander of the Star on India) in 1936 for his meritorious services. As a great ruler, he remained a highly reputed and powerful administrator throughout his life. Jubbal Royal family has its own importance in the history Indian Princely states.

His Youngest son, Late Lt. Col. Raj Kumar Virendra Singh was one of the earliest commissioned officers of the British Indian Army who fought for his country Overseas during the Second World War of 1939-45. It was his son Kunwar Uday Singh who converted Woodville Palace into a Heritage Hotel in 1977. India is a country of multi cultural and socio - religious life. The Heritage tourism may gain new momentum in the country in the coming years. The Woodville Palace Resorts has set marvellous examples to encourage heritage tourism in the country.

Business men's world: The another Royal cottage in the premises has two luxury suites. The tourists enjoy excellent food, drinks and all facilities in a peaceful environment. It becomes more comfortable after lunch when we have a glass of fresh orange juice and relax in the Golden Tiger Lounge. Here, we can see a galaxy of photographs signed by the Hollywood stars of the glorious era of 1930s. The elite class enjoy billiards, table tennis and badminton in the resort.

In all, the Woodville Palace Resorts is a peaceful paradise. It is most useful for business meetings, successful planning, conferences, group meetings, corporate world discussions and social events and seminars. This Palace Resorts has become a VIPS stay point in Shimla Hills.

Nature's Paradise: The Palace is something more sophisticated for bird watching, site seeing and relaxing into the lap of mother nature. The air is cool and clear, sunrise and sunsets are quite remarkable. Night skies are bedecked with stars and in spring, the lawns are ablaze with sweet smelling flowers.

Pastures and Valleys: The beautiful roads, mountains passes and traverse valleys, grassy meadows in a region that has much to offer trout anglers, hikers and nature lovers. Giri Ganga, Jubbal, Taalraa-Chaupal, Chanshal-Rohdu are the best pastures lands to explore.

Winter Adventures: Shimla is rich in scenic splendour, particularly in winter after snow fall. Kupped and Khara Pather areas provide wonderful trekking opportunities a challenge for the fit and energetic.

Nature Watcher's Paradise: In modern times, Shimla Hills are famous for nature watching, bird watching and snow landscape studies. The nature lovers from far and wide come here to relax into the lap of mother nature.

TARADEVI FORESTS: A RESPITE FOR SUMMER

The Tara Devi Forests are nature's wonderland. The whole Tara Devi Forest land is a beautiful place to explore and enjoy life afresh. The deodar trees, Oak trees and Pine trees are assembled into most enchanting fashion. It is an unique example of a mixed forests. The Pine trees are found at the low heights. We can calculate the height of a place seeing the growth of Deodara cedarus, Oak and pinus. There is a beautiful temple at the top of Tara Devi mountain and is managed by the Cultural Department of Himachal Government.

The pedestrial path going to Tara Devi is quite pleasant, full of peace and, serenity. For us it was an adventurous experience in itselt as it passed through the dense forests and the mountaineous slopes known for its silppery nature. The Tara Devi Bus Stop is seven kilometers from Shimla. From Tara Devi Bus Stop we can trek on foot upto the mountain temple of Tara Devi which is at 7 or 8 kilometers in distance. It is an adventurous but most enjoyable journey in the summer days.

The winter days are harsh and it may be quite difficult for some people who are not habitual of trekking over such a mountain terrains.

The Expedition to Tara Devi: Tara Devi is a peaceful natrual resort to enjoy life during summer as well as winter. But summer days are full of golden happiness and enthralling. Tara Devi forests and valleys are full of shade and natural beauty. There is a beautiful growth of wild flowers in Tara Devi mountains and forestlands and grassland are quite impressive. The slippery pathways are quite adventurous and pleasant during the months of summer as well as winter. The summer months are quite pleasant and full of enjoyment while the winter is harsh and difficult in the forests. But the rooms inside Dharmshala remain quite warm. The pilgrims, devotees and trekkers visit here regularly whether it is snowclad or it is raining. The people have a great respect and devotion to Tara Devi the mother Goddess. They worship Gods and Goddesses inside the temples. The pilgrims come in thousands and the whole environment is full of religious and spiritual activities. The religious tourism in the Tara Devi Resorts is in peak season from March to September-October. The winter months also remain full of religious activities but due to harsh winds the old people rarely visit the temple. But for youngsters enjoy it as a kind of thrill.

After visiting the temple and the Tara Devi Mountain Peak we can proceed towards lowlands below three kilometers from Tara Devi. That's Lord Mahadev Temple in the foot hills of Tara Devi known as the most ancient temple and the religious resorts of the Tara Devi Valley. The temple and the Dharmshala here make it most peaceful and enjoyable place in the Shimla Hills. The temple of Lord Shiva was constructed in the time of Raja Shri Mahendra Sen, the powerful ruler of Junga State. Shri Mahendra Sen was known for his goodwill, charity, peoples well wisher, social welfare schemes and more to that he was a great lover of temples and the religious activities in the area. He was avid trekker, explorers and a keen lovers of nature.

The Mahendra Sen Resort in Tara Devi is famous for its multipurpose tourism and exploration activities. From here, we can establish base camp and we can explore various places of religious, social, anthropological and cultural importance. From

Raja Mahandra Sen Resort, we can have the clear cut views of Junga State, surrounding mountains, valleys, villages and forests. For several cultural and religious festivals, we can approach to nearby villages where we can study cultural, religious and social life of its citizens.

From Raja Mahendra Sen Resort, we can proceed on to the heights of Tara Devi mountain peaks and can have the beautiful glimpses of the villagers, valleys, orchards and forests with a distinct vision of natural beauty.

The Resort is also famous for the purpose of meditation, living in solitude, study and writing in loneliness. The place is more loving and inspiring particularly for the writers, journalists, poets, novelists and the nature lovers.

Nature's Peaceful Paradise: The Raja Mahendra Resort is quite famous for nature watching, exploration and bird watching. Here we can have the beautiful glimpses of the natural landscapes, trees, plants and medicinal herbs. The summer days are full of romance and thrill.

In the middle of the valley there is a beautiful Tara Devi Resorts famous for film shooting and tourism activities in the area. The Tara Devi Resort, is quite old one and has some British period of cottages which earlier were of British Army officer and now punchased by an Indian businessman. The location is beautiful and full of flowers of different varieties.

The flowering genders of Tara Devi Resorts are quite popular among the tourists, trekkers travellers and mountaineers. This resort is a peaceful paradise for nature lovers. It is surrounded by dense forests and beautiful mountain slopes. The Tara Devi Resort is a man-made well developed resort built for multipurpose activities on most modern lines. As it has a splendid cottage, swimming pool, rest house and an Hawa Mahal for good summer days. This the best place for film shooting and get to gather.

On the other hand, The Raja Mahendra Sen Resort is mend for religious, spiritual and educational activities as the temple here is considered the most ancient period. Later on the Raja Mahendra Sen built the temple on his efforts for the purpose of local pilgrims and nature lovers. The resort and the temple complex have multipurpose aim:

(*a*) To keep in mind the people's emotional attachments to their Gods and Goddesses.

(*b*) The place is famous among the nature lovers and is known among the nature watchers from far and near.

(*c*) ***The Trekker's Playground:*** The trekkers, climbers and wild plant lovers come from far and near to enjoy the trekking and the beauty of wild plants in the area.

(*d*) Explorers and camp lovers most favoured destination; Raja Mahendra Sen was known for his affection for forests and pastures. He used to spend nights in the open forests for his experience and enjoyment. The area is known for best exploration and camplife activities.

(*e*) ***Oak-forest and Water Well:*** The most fascinating and amazing thing is that we had located an oak-root water stream which is too cold to drink during the hot summers. The valley is dominated by oak, rhododendron, deodar, Kail and pine trees and remains cool and pleasant during the months of summer. The wild land is full of wild flowers and aromatic plants and is the real heaven for the botanists, environmentalists and plant lovers during summer.

The Orchid Lovers Paradise: Tara Devi Wilderness is a fascinating one and is the home of several species of terrestrial orchids, mountain lilies, mini sunflowers, varbascum longifoliam, Lisimachia, Punctata, Leotopodium alpinum, lupia, Pathar chutta, kamalia ((Bergenia Ciliata), larksper and several aromatic plants and herbs.

The larger species of common oak with beautiful large nuts is found in Tara Devi. The whole mountain is an example of mixed forests of Deodar cedarus, kail, oak, pinus, and several other local dwarf trees, plants and thorny buses. Some beautiful wild flower bushes and hanging plants are found in the forests. Among the orchids, common terrestrial orchids with yellow green flowers are found in the mountain peaks. The exotic lady's slipper and pinkesh flowering orchids are found is the surrounding of Tara Devi forest land. At the top of the mountains, the wild rose locally known as "Kujai" is found in abunance. The white flowers of this rose family bush blossom during summer and are full of sweet fragrance. In the evening and morning the environment near the flowering bushes is filled with scented smell. It becomes more enjoyable when the cool breeze welcomes us in the hot summer days at the top of the peak.

Besides orchids, there are several varieties of Lisimachia punctata or feunladi in the wild. This is the most beautiful exciting wild green bush which gives bright yellow flowers during April to August. There are four main species of this multipurpose flowering bush in Tara Devi hills.

Among them are:

1. Giant bushes of feunladi, which provides numerous small yellow flowers. It is around six feet in height. It is extensively ornamental.
2. Domestic feunladi, mostly found near the gardens and agriculture fields of the village people. It is also present near the corners of barren land and apple orchards within shady environment. The flowers are very delicate and fall after two three days.
3. Peedhi or Bright yellow feunladi is known for its wild exciting wild flowers which are sharp yellow in colour and shine brightly during the bright sun. This is the most exciting species of feunladi (Lisimachia Punctata) and is known for its multipurpose medicinal values. It is a quick remedy for cut and burn injurries and moles. It is used in old injury, breast cancer, hair falling, for the brightness of face (used in the form of paste and herbal masc) and in every kind of body aches. In many ways, this herb is called the "Sanjeevani" of the mountain people. We should protect the feunladi and reproduce it in the wild and use it in herbal medicines. Skin diseases, moles and serval other injuries are cured by this unique herb. It can be grown at home as the ornamental plant.

The mountain resorts, world over have become a great source of holiday, health and eco-tourism activities. The

Nalagarh Heritage Resort is the most popular among the businessmen and budget tourists in India and abroad. The fort is 800 years old established on a beautiful hill.

There are some outstanding hotels resorts, nature resorts and health tourism resorts in the country. Himachal, Uttaranchal, Rajasthan and Kerala have become most popular for tourist resorts.

In Rajasthan Rohet Garh Hotel Resorts has become quite popular among the visitors worldwide. The seventeenth century palace has been converted into a Hotel Resorts by Thakur Mahendra Singh. The Resort is 40 kilometers from Jodhpur in Rohet Garh. Pop-singer Madona has made this resort her destination in January 2008. The resort is best example of modern hotel resorts in the country.

19

Conservation of Orchid Forests of Dehradun

The most beautiful wild lands in the world are vanishing away gradually. Some of the orchid forests in the world have been disappeared because of global warming, continuous population growth, deforestation and increasing air and water pollution. This has caused a grave concern among the orchid lovers worldwide.

We have lost 30% of Amazonia wilderness, a large part of Malaysia forests and some Indonesian forests have been lost in the last one decade. Some important orchid species from the world have disappeared because of ruthless deforestation in several countries.

If the governments of the concerned countries of the world do not take proper step to halt such maladies, the orchid forests of the world will vanish away soon. The Toya River orchid forests, Chidderwala, Dehradun, (Uttaranchal) Tharoch valley terrestrial orchids in Himachal, Nagarja Pakha orchids, Simtoli in Pauri hills have become endangered because of continuous deforestation and global warming.

Some of the orchid forests of the world are on the verge of extinction and some of them have already been vanished away because of the disappearance of swamp areas and other climatic diversions. In past one century the swamp forests of Chidderwala have been reduced from 80 Square km. to four square km. This climatic change has resulted into the disappearance of orchid forests and fresh water mangroves of Chidderwala in Dehradun. Orchids, are a very strange world of flowers known for their graceful beauty and colour combinations as well. The orchids are found in various parts of the world and are of both ornamental and medicinal values.

One of the best and oldest ornamengal plant hobbies, orchid culture now enjoy worldwide popularity. The incredible beauty and diversity of orchids captivate men and women from all walks of life. Because of its varieties the orchids are exported by their cultivators all over the world. In India, we can earn a handsome foreign exchange by exporting orchids if the government takes some concrete steps to encourage higher study and research on the most fabulous species of this exotic flower.

According to a report of American Orchid Society, approximately 35,000 species of orchids that grow around the world, none of them is parasitic. They are found in every country of the world from South Africa to Alaska (USA). The orchids are classified as aerophytic epiphytes, lithophytes, Saprophytes and terrestrials.

American Orchid Society, a group of more than 10,0000 people worldwide is continuously providing the meticulous information on orchid culture. This is the most popular organisation to disseminate the information to orchid lovers. The most populor orchids species of the world are Paphiopedilum Sukhakulli, dendrobium cuthbertsonie, masdevallia, dendrobium Pinkysem, Sophrolaeliocattleya, Phalaenopsis Little Mary, Disa Helmut Meyer, Brassolaelio Cattelya San Diego, Cymbidium Via Mar Tranghila Christina Dendrobium Ekapol, Massdevallia, Oncidium Taka, Paphiopedilum faire, Phalaenopsis Little Richard, Vanda Piyaporn are among the most beautiful orchids in the world.

In India, blue, violet, yellow and white orchids are most popular qualities for export. There is a great need to develop the orchidacies in various parts of the country. The Government and the NGOS should do their best to cultivate orchids for exports and the orchid lovers should be trained with great efforts.

Presently, there are some orchid nurseries in Calcutta, Bombay and Bangalore to cultivate and breed exotic qualities of colourful orchids for interior decoration as well as for export. At the same time, the orchid technicians can get employment in a large number. The unemployed educated and trained youth can be absorbed in various orchid farms in the country. Presently, Bangalore is very successful place in growing orchids at commercial scale.

Seeing the importance of orchid culture, the proper steps should be taken for its conservation all over the world. For example, International Institute of Mountain Studies and Research, New Delhi with the co-operation of International Orchid Club, Chidderwala Dehradun, is protecting the swamp areas and orchid forests of Chidderwala. The above organisations are first of its kind in the country which have made the history to protect the above forests rich in bio-diversity. The NGOS should come forward to protect the other plant species and bio-diversity all over the world. American Orchids Society and Fauna and Flora International UK have done their best to protect the important plant species in various parts of the world. The FFI, UK provides excellent financial support for every project.

The Ministry of Agriculture has established some Orchid Research Centres in the North East but with limited resources. Ours is an amazing and varied plant kingdom with exotic orchid species and we should do our best to conserve, protect it and grow it at commercial scale. Unfortunately, the Orchid Research Centres have not done expected work in the field of orchid research and conservation. Some NGOs have taken the initiative but without financial resources they have proved like a pious hope. In this way, the Government should think about this with positive look and the business houses should finance the NGOs involved in the orchid research and conservation activities.

The Swamp Forests of Dehradun: The swamp forests of Dehradun are known for their rich bio-diversity. The forest has a rich composition of Orchid species *i.e.,* Obenoria and Vanda Cristata. These Orchid species have attracted the botanists, ecologists and orchid lovers the world over. The swamp forests are fresh water mangroves widely known for their beautiful orchid species and different kinds of plants. The freshwater aromatic plants and herbs have their peculier characteristics of sub-tropical environment in these waters. The sweet-plant (saunf) is known for its sweet taste and smell. The swamp forests of Toya river, Gola Tapper are the best examples of epiphyte orchids in the area and should be conserved with great interest and efforts.

There is a great need for the research and study of these orchid species and the conservation activities in the swamp forests. The Forest Research Institute has done very outstanding work in the areas of orchid species collection and research work. We should not satisfy ourselves with this small research and try our best to explore more avenues in orchid collection and research. The other orchid Research Centres and botanical institutes in the country have done a very outstanding work in the conservation of various plant species in the country. The colleges and universities should also take some good steps to mobilise their resources for botanical research in the country. P. G. Degree College, Rishikesh has done an outstanding work on the Flora of Shivalik Hills and Swamp Forests of Dehradun, Dr. Som Deva and Dr. Govind Rajwar have done some admirable work in this regard. The worst thing to happen is that these swamp forests have been reduced a mere 3 to 4 kilometers while they were spread upto 80 square km about a century ago. Ecological findings say that the denudation of forests and encroachment of land has destroyed any chance of their survival. A new NGO, the International Institute of Mountains Studies and Research is doing outstanding work for the conservation of orchid forests of Dehradun and other parts of India. At present, the project in conservation of orchid forests is continuing in Dehradun, Sikkim and Khasi hills. A mass awareness campaign is already in existence. The PTA's and the schools have joined hands for the protection and conservation of orchid forests in the Shivalik hills in Dehradun district.

There are two main species of orchids found in the swamp forests of Gola Tappar (Chidderwala), Dehradun. The leaves of these two sub-tropical orchid species are highly fleshy and shine with the compact food material stored in them. The most interesting orchid species, Obenoria, has such shining leaves. It is the most delicate orchid in the region.

The tropical orchids are epiphytic, meaning that they attach themselves to trees. They are not parasites because they process their own food deriving nutrients and moisture from the air through their aerial roots. Vanda cristata is an epiphyte ornamental herb with leaf and stem which often climbs the branches of mango, saal, bassia and letifolia (mahua) trees. The stem of Vanda Cristata is harder then Obenoria, long in comparison, the roots are aerial linear, 1-5 inches long, fruit and capsul form, seeds are minute, non-endospermic and embroyo is indifferentiate.

What is the economic importance of orchids? The orchids have the most developed and advanced flower systems in the world. Due to their remarkable colour, forms and profusion, it makes them a favourite with florists and horticulturists. Many genera and their hybrids are cultivated as ornamental plants. The notables among these are cypripedium cattleya, habeneria, bletilla, vanda, cypripedium, dendrobium, epidendrum, epipactis, coelogyne, and aerides.

The capsule of Vanilla fragrance ames syn. Vanilla planifolia (Vanilla) and several other species of this tropical genus are the source of Vanilla which is extensively used for flavouring various food products i.e. coffee, icecream and various sweets etc. The tubers of Platenthera sussannae (L) Lind Syn. Habeneria Sussannae are edible. The dried tuberous roots of Orchids latifolia L. used as a farinaceous food and nervine tonic. It is also used in sizing material in silk industry. Salepa is a common drink produced from Cymbidium aloifolium Swatz. Wild Orchids are used in costly perfumes and other herbal beauty items. In several African countries some orchid species are used as life saving medicines and some as food items in Malaysia. One species of orchid is used as talisman to keep the evils away. Tribals in North - East Asia and some African countries eat the raw tubers of some orchids.

Once the orchids were very costly flowers but now they are everybody's favourite. In 1885, according to Horticulture Encylopaedia, the prices of orchids went up to US $ 500 a plant. The orchids are largest families of flowering plants on earth. It is estimated that there are 15,000 to 35,000 orchid species under 400 to 800 genera in the world. Some of the root tubers of orchids are similar to 'Orchis' or testicles (Gr. Orchis-testicles) hence orchid. It is discovered that orchids will not germinate unless the seeds become infested with mycorhizal fungus. The tiny seedlings live saprophytically during early part of their life, as they don't have any food resource of their own.

Many tropical orchids like Vanda, Aerides etc. are grown best into the suspended baskets. The medium in which plants are grown is a mixture of osmonds and sphagnum moss. Adequate drainage and appropriate temperature are critical to successful cultivation of orchids. The ecological nature of orchids is quite strange. They are found from the icy Alaska to the forests of Borneo. The world's best orchids species are found in South and Central America, India and Sri Lanka. Most of the attractive species of Orchids are found in Myanmar, Indonesia, Thailand Philippines, New Guinea and Australia. The Fiji Islands and Jamaica are the most suitable places for the growth of such orchids.

There has been a lot of research work on orchids. The International Orchid Society of India (IOS) and American Orchid Society (AOS) have done a lot of survey and research work independently. IOSI is leading in the conservation of orchid forests in India as well as abroad through orchid conservation awareness programmes. AOS is conducting a number of surveys and research works as it has proper resources and financial assets to conduct the projects all over the world. The other orchid organisations are also in good form to run the conservation projects in their respective countries. i.e. The Amateur Orchid Growers Society, Orchid Council of New Zealand, Dutch Orchid Society, British Orchid Society, Orchid Society of Jamaica. Orchid Society of Switzerland, Orchid Society of Mauritius, and Northern Ireland has done a good deal of work in the field of conservation.

There is a great need to encourage higher research and survey work and conservation of orchids in developing countries. IOSI and International Institute of Mountain Studies and Research (IIMSR) are doing their best in the field of conservation of Orchid forests in India as well as abroad. Presently, they have concentrated on the North-Western Himalayas and the North-Eastern parts of India. The above societies are doing their best to save the endangered ecosystems of the Sunderban mangroves also. IIMSR has established 1000 orchid conservation clubs in the mountain regions of Himachal,

Uttaranchal, Sikkim and Khasi hills with the support of parents, teachers and students. Such conservation clubs are co-operating the mass awareness campaigns to save the orchid forests of the country.

Presently, the orchid is grown and cultivated on commercial scale in Canada, UK, USA, Australia, Newzealand Thailand and other Coastal island nations where the environment is most suitable for their natural growth. In India too, we should make it a movement and have our own orchid culture. This is the most impressive flower in the world and we should do our best to cultivate and propagate orchid species on a larger commercial scale.

Orchids for Tourism: The orchid forests of the world have become immense attraction among the tourists, trekkers and botanists the world over. The orchid forests of Peru, Brazil and Central America are quite fascinating and full of natural beauty.

The City of Orchids: The forests of Peru is known for its beautiful orchids. Its has a district and the state named Moyobamba. This is the capital city San Martin Region, has a population of 50,000 and the orchid species 3,500. Moyobamba is called the city of orchids and is quite popular among the travellers all over the world.

Economic Importance: Orchid have a great economic importance as they are the commercial flowers. Tulip orchids have become the most profitable crop of orchid flowers the world over. Thailand, New Zealand, Japan, Philippines grow tulips.

In India, Sikkim is called the "State of orchids". Both terrestrial and epiphytes. In 1818 William Cattley became the first person to bloom orchid, an event that changed the flower world forever. For centuries orchid have been a symbol of love, luxury and beauty. In the 19th century orchids were auctioned at 500 pound for a single plant.

Vanilla for Export: Vanilla orchids are known for their commercial values. Its cultivation was first introduced in Central America in 1800. It is an important crop in much of the tropics.

Vanilla of Madagaskar: Madagaskar is the leading producer of Vanilla orchids. In alone in 2005, it produced 3 million metric tonnes (of a world total 7.3 million metric tonnes) the Coca cola company is the world's largest user of Vanilla. Besides, its use as a flavouring it is also used in fragrances and perfumes. Vanilla is a very labour intensive crop since the flowers have to be pollinated by hand. It is considered as one of the most profitable enterprizes for small family farms.

The taxonomy of this family is in constant flux, as DNA studies give new information. An indepth treatment of the taxonomy is given in the Taxonomy of the orchid family.

There are more than 800 genera in orchidacae family.

The Orchid flora of North West Himalaya : A British officer John Firminger Duthie (1845-1922) was the Director of Botanic Department, Northern India. He wrote an outstanding report on the flora Orchids of North-Western Himalaya in 1906. He gave an account of 173 species and illustrated some 53 of them.

A century has passed since then and the detailed information on the studies of orchids given by Duthie is an excellent one. The area which Duthie covered in these days is divided now into India and Pakistan.

The present work on Orchids includes 239 species, more than 66 of Duthie's flora.

The earliest record of Orchid collection in the Garhwal Himalaya goes back to 1796 initiated by Major-General Thomas Hardwick. In the beginning of the 19th century William Spencer Webb an officer of Bengal Engineers and surveyor of first rank collected plants from Jamnotri, Gangotri, Kali river on the boundary of Kumaon and Nepal. Sir. J.D. Hooker's studies of the orchids of India were published in 1890. Seiden faden (73, 1973) has very correctly mentioned that Hooker was the most clear minded taxonomist and his work stands even today a hundred years later as the main source of knowledge and his taxonomic judgements have stood the ravages of time. His coverage on Orchids of the North Western Himalaya was based on the result of an extensive exploration of Orchid forests.

20

Nature Tourism : Transformation And Development

The natural areas all over the world are being protected for the development of nature tourism. The high budget tourists all over the world visit the most precious natural lands in the world. Such beautiful lands, are full of bio-diversity, wetlands, rich in floral diversity and wildbirds. To encourage the tourists and scholars to such places is called nature tourism. There are several hundred beautiful natural sites all over the world which can be preserved for the recreation and enjoyment of future generation. Some of them will disappear in the coming one century. We, the citizens of the earth should protect its environment by all positive means. Unfortunately, 30 percent of world's most beautiful scenic lands have been disfigured or disappeared from this earth. There are so many planets and stars in the universe but they all are without life and full of harsh environment. The earth is the only planet which is full of greenergy and most suitable to human beings and wild life.

The Vanishing Natural Lands

In the past one century several forests, wild lands, wilderness, wetlands and heathlands have been disappeared because of agricultural development and growing population. The rapid urbanisation and colonisation has receded the size of natural areas.

The natural lands have been affected by the growing population and their encroachment for housing, agriculture, resorts, ranches and farm houses. Such activities have reduced agricultural, forest and natural lands.

The wetlands and their eco-system has been effected by the global warming, pollution and development activities.

The Famous Grasslands

The following natural lands have been worst affected by now :

(1) The coastal plains, (2) Dambo, (3) Deserts, (4) Field, (5) Flooded grasslands and savannas, (6) Flood meadows, (7) Llanos, (8) Meadows, (9) Pampa, (10) Pastures, (11) Plains, (12) Plateaus, (13) Praries, (14) Savannas, (15) Steppe, (16) Taiga, (17) Tundra, (18) Veld, (19) water meadow, (20) wet meadow.

The Future of Wetlands

The freshwater lakes all over the world are disappearing very fast. The waterlands of Mexico, Brazil, Borneo, Philippines, Papua New Guini are on the verge of reduction. Global warming, growing population and pollution have affected them gravely. It is seen that important grasslands, typical forests, wildlands and wetlands have been worst effected by the global warming, pollution and development in the past one century. There is a great need to protect them by all positive means.

Paradise Park, Jamaica is full of pastures and bright scenic views. A great number of wild flowering plants and shrubs are found there.

There is a beautiful U Tube River forelands Dessel. There are some most beautiful flowering pastures along the banks of river Dessal. This is called a river of beauty and prosperity.

The flowering pastures are a characteristic of Australian continent. The continent is full of vast wildlands, expanded wilderness and most enchanting forest lands in the world

The Tropical Forests of Australia

The tropical forests of Australia are evergreen and more enchanting in the world. From rain forests, to open pastures, create a heaven on earth. The explorer and trekkers have enjoyed their most beautiful days in the pastures of Australia. The huge trees, large bushes, long grass, dwarf trees and wild flowers impress all of us. The ferns and orchids of Australia are quite popular the world over. Dicksonia Antarctica (Soft tree fern) is found in Greensland, and Australia. There are amazing fern trees in Australia from 15 meters to 25 meters in height.

Cyathea cunninghamii (slender fern tree), cyathea cooperi, Christella dentala are among the beautiful tree ferns.

The Evergreen Wildlands

In Himachal and Uttaranchal (India) there are amazing pastures and scenic wildlands quite popular among the trekkers, explorers and botanists of the world. The nature lover come to these places into a large numbers. The Taatraa Pastures (Tharoch), Kupped Pastures, Tumroo Table land, (Jubbal), Chaanshal Valley Pastures, Rohdu, all are in Shimla district of Himachal Pradesh. These pastures are nature's peaceful paradise and are among the most beautiful scenic places of the country.

Taalraa Pastures are heaven and amazingly attract the explorer and trekkers from far and near. The flowering pastures are most impressive in the world.

The meadows and flowering pastures : The flowering pastures of Canada and South Africa have become the best places of nature tourism in the world. In South Africa, there is a pasture valley of flowers which amazingly attracts the tourists in large numbers. In India the Valley of flowers in Chamoli and Flowering Pasture Chaanshal are best known among the trekkers and explorers of the world.

The Amazonian Wilderness

The vast rain forests of Amazonia are spread upto 40 lakh square kilometers. These are the largest wilderness in the world after Antarctica. Antarctica is the largest wilderness covered with snow and with human population.

The Amazonia wilderness is spread along the river Amazon and its tributaries. These are the best rain forests in the world and are called the lungs of the earth as they provide maximum oxygen and absorb CO_2 from the environment. The two thirds of the world's rain forests exist in Amazonia.

The deforestation in Brazilian Amazon has increased by 27 per cent in 1998, 16,800 square km. have been cleared. Since 1972, 532,068 sq. km., 13.3 per cent of entire Amazon region has been lost. 10000 to 15000 sq. km. forests are destroyed by the logging crew every year. It is estimated that by 1987, some

204,000 sq. km. of rain forest were burned to clear land for agriculture.

British Meadows and Pastures

Seventy five percent of flower rich meadows known for their existence in Peak District National Park, UK in 1980s have either been lost completely or have suffered serious decline in their plant diversity. Apparently, in their current national agri environment mechanism and incentives are insufficient to halt such losses. Since last five years in the county of Herdfordshire the meadows have disappearing gradually.

The Pantanal Wetland

Pantanal wetlands is the largest in the world expanding upto 2,10000 sq. km. around the Uberaba lake in Brazil. The wetland is the home of 60,000 marsh deers and several other mammals *i.e.* tigers, bears, wildpigs, crocodiles, caiman, snakes and tortoise. Within this wetland, there are several iron are companies operating in the area. Pantanal wetlands have a distinct eco-system of their own similar to other tropical forests and wetlands. In this vast wetland, several farm houses, ranches and agro-business based farming industry in operating for the past several years.

The Camargue

Camargue wetland is a finest examples of protected wetland at the mouth of Rone river in Southern France. It covers 850 sq. km. of sandysoil, marshes and shallow lakes, with a patch work of grassland and scrub between the waterways. The beach stretches over 100 km.

Camargue is famous for its natural beauty and scenic landscapes. It is a well known habitat for the birds and is one of the three most important wetlands in Europe. This is the breeding place of Flamingos, herons, ducks, bee eators and several other bird species. This is the main resting place for 300 species of migrating birds.

To protect the area further, there is a state Nature Reserve in the middle of the park which is even more carefully controlled. Its 13,000 hectares is open to the scholars, scientists and biologists for the study and research work.

Camargue is a rich rice growing area—producing 100000 tonnes of rice per year. Rice is grown under water and the rice fields drain into the central reserve causing changes in the depth and saltiness of the water. Camargue is a multipurpose wetland useful for the citizens as well as farmers of France. In some way, this is the best use of a wetland.

Most Beautiful Natural Lands of the World: There are some beautiful scenic lands and natural areas in the world useful for the purpose of Eco-tourism and exploration activities. India tops the list.

1. Great Himalayan National Park, Kullu : This National Park is a heaven for mountain birds. It is estimated that in the year round 300 bird species come to this park and after same time fly away to other destinations. The birds permanently seen here are : Western Himalayans Tragopan (Tragopan Melavo Cephalus); Monal (Lophorus Impejanus), Small Monal (Catereus Wallichi), Koklas-Pucrasia Macrolopha, and Kaleej Pheasant : Lophura Leucomelona, the Himalayan Crowned cock. (Tetragullus Himalayensis) is also found in the upper hights. Kullu national Park is the Nature's peaceful paradise. It is rich both in flora and fauna.

2. Rajaji National Park : The amazing wilderness Rajaji National Park is known for its vast expansion and rich bio-diversity. For example the Asian elephants, leopard, tigers, bears, neel gai, wildpigs, stag, marsh deers, brown-red fox, rabit, shahi, wild cats (Gothoo) are found here. Among the reptiles water snake, king kobra, python, diamond back; black spot snake are found here. Among the birds, Pankaua (Red Crow), water foul, wild fowl, common crow, turtle dove, white crane, fish Cacher (Bagula), white crane, king fisher, yellow bird, chanchud, karawoon (magpie) and other 65 species of birds are found here.

3. The Grassy Wildlands of Spain : The pastures of Spain are known for their famous grassland, beautiful rocks and dwarf trees. The islands of Spain are most beautiful assets of nature tourism in the world. Mallorca, Ibiza and Menogra islands are in medi-terrenean sea and full of scenic beauty. Spain has become a destination of international tourists. The population of spain is 40 million and in a year round 50 million international and national tourists visit Spain. This has boosted the economy of spain in tourism.

4. Island of Halmahera : Indonesian island of Halmahera has been converted into a National Park after a longtime decision. The Park will protect 167,300 ha of hill and low land. It will save 23 bird species including Cuckoo shriek and other amazing birds. It will also save the life of roaming tribals Tobelo Dalam whose life was disturbed by continuing logging and deforestation.

5. Sable Islands (Nova Scotia, Canada) is a 40 km long crescent of sand off east coast of Nova Scoti Islands. Among other things, the island supports largest beautiful colony of grey seals (halichoerus grypus) and one of the biggest mixed species of terns in Canada. Canada government is supporting a research work on Sable island and its water animals.

The Foya Mountains

A team of scientists have found the most ancient unexplored forests in Asia. The Foya Mountains are the most isolated forests in the Western New Guinea. There are a few dozens of new species of honey enters, 20 frog species and four butterflies species, the expeditions also obtained the first photographs of the spectacular Berlepsch six-wired bird paradise, thereby confirming the location of the range of this remarkable species. The interiors of the Foya Mountains range, which consists of more than 300000 ha of old growth of tropical forests. This is an Endemic Bird Area and an ideal place of bird studies.

Taxa, The New Zealand Plants

New Zealand is known for its rich bio-diversity in the world. 80% of countries vascular plants are endemic. For the past some decades the flora has been on decline an in recent conservation assessment from vascular plant taxa were listed as extinct and 119 as acutely threatened. A further 102 taxa are seriously at risk and 502 taxa are at risk. The New Zealand Plant Conservation Network, botanists and NGO save supporting conservation work in New Zealand with the support of Government Department of Conservation. The taxa plants land is beautiful for nature studies.

New aspects of Nature Tourism

Nature tourism has been proliferated into several branches as eco-tourism and wildlife. Eco-tourism denotes tourism related to ecology or environment. Nature conservation and environmental studies go together.

Eco-Tourism

Eco-tourism is a new subject in tourism and is hardly twenty six years old. It was initiated in some countries in 1980. In 2002, United Nations celebrated International Year of Eco-tourism. The meeting was a watershed event. It was created with those who pioneered and encouraged tourism in the wild lands in the world. According to Heather Robinson (2006), it is a subject of sustainable tourism, differing by its focus on ecology. Eco-Tourism is sustainable tourism that "contributes actively to the conservation of natural and cultural heritage."

Wildlife Tourism

Wildlife tourism attracts a large number of tourists from different countries. For example the wild life of Kruger National Park, South Africa and/Wildlife Parks of Uganda, Kenya and Zimbabwe, are doing well in wildlife tourism. The wild life of Amazonia Borneo-Sumatra, Papua New Guinea, Australia, and Indian Natural Parks are an excellent example of wildlife tourism and attract a large number of international tourists.

Cultural Heritage

The ancient monuments, temples, ancient cities, forts, and idols are some of the findings in some countries are known as the culture heritage. The people go to see the temple of Borubudur Ankorbat. There are Lord Budha's largest images in Afghanistan and Takshshila in Pakistan. The tourists visit these sites in large numbers and enjoy the architecture of relics.

Natural Heritage

The most beautiful scenic spots in this world has been brought under world Natural Heritage. There are several thousand pastures, valleys, rivers, wetlands and forests which are most ancient and rare in nature and are known as the natural heritage on the earth. We should protect such places of human interest. The UNESCO Natural Heritage department has listed them among the rare and most beautiful natural sites in the world.

Wilderness Tourism

The wilderness tourism has become quite popular in UK, Canada and Brazil and adjoining countries where there are largest pasture, meadows and flowering river banks.

At present Canada's British Columbia is an amazing state full of natural lands in the forms of valleys, pastures, meadows, forests and wilderness. British Columbia has become world leader in wilderness tourism. There are some twenty companies in Canada, USA and Brazil which are sponsoring and operating a large number of tours to Amazonia.

Amazonia wilderness is known for its amazing wildlife, mammals, bird fauna, reptiles and butterflies etc. World's one fifth of birds are found in the Great Wilderness of Amazonia. It is certain that the wildlife lovers will visit these rain forests of human importance.

The Famous Grasslands

The famous grasslands world over have become the passion for trekkess and explorers. For example, the meadows in Canada, Australia, Denmark, Sweden and Switzerland have become quite popular among the people of the world.

The fern trees in New South Wales of Australia and Tasmania have became popular sites among the nature lovers worldwide.

British Columbia

British columbia is the most beautiful state of Canada which is known for beautiful wildlands, wetlands, forests and pastures. Canada government is earning maximum revenue from tourism from this state. British Columbia is the best example of nature tourism and wilderness tourism in the world.

British Columbia Super Natural Parks and vast areas of wilderness are attracting more tourists every year. This country has made wilderness tourism a rapidly expanding industry.

There are twenty wilderness tourism companies in Canada and USA which are most active in the tourism in British Columbia. Besides this, Wilderness Tourism Association is doing a lot of efforts to encourage tourism and the same time to preserve the nature of British Columbia.

At present, British Columbia is the key economic driver for the Canada government and those business houses who are sponsoring the wilderness travel and tours through their companies.

Nature Tourism (Wilderness Tourism) is the fastest growing sector in in USA, Canada, Brazil, South Africa and has done a lot of good work to attract nature lovers worldwide.

In 2001, wilderness tourism generated US $ 900 million in direct revenues. The spin offs and indirect revenue generated from travel to and from nature based operations. The total revenue was 2 billion US $ and 21,000 people got full time jobs in 2001. The other small job holders also got work in the industry.

At represent time, British Columbia is a leader in global tourism market place. But the future of this worldclass tourism product depends on the secure land base. This issue is the key question in British Columbia land use management practices.

Wilderness Tourism and Key Factors :

1. Environment Protection
2. Regional Economic Health
3. Supportive Relationship with Local Communities
4. Impacts on Local Culture
5. Quality Guest Experiences.

Longtime viability of wilderness tourism operation can be achieved through conservation, management and research in the following areas :

1. Advocacy on key wilderness tourism issues and operations.
2. Development of best practices in the profession.
3. Proper expertisation in wilderness Tourism Training.
4. Related Research Work for the Newcomers.
5. The role of communication and media agencies. Its proper utilization in protecting and publicising the beautiful natural areas.

6. The role of Wilderness Tourism Association organisations and organizational development.

Coastal Tourism

Coastal Tourism has given new economic achievements to USA. Presently USA is the major beneficiary of international tourism in which is the most expanding economic sector in the world today. It is estimated that in 1995, US earned 746 billion dollars. Travel and tourism in USA is fastly improving than the earlier decades. The USA travel industry is providing jobs to 14.4 million people annually. The US manufacturing industries from IBM to General Motors provide employment to only 18 million people. The 85 per cent of all tourist revenues are earned by coastal states and 90 per cent of all tourists. Spending occurs in these states (Houston 1996). The coastal areas of Northern Europe, Mediterranean, Caribbean beaches, Gold Coasts of Australia and Fiji are among the very attractive beaches. Hawaii coastal tourism is becoming more popular among the tourists of the world.

Mountain Tourism

Mountain tourism is quite popular among the regional and international tourists. The mountaineers, trekkers and explorers have a great affection for Indian mountains. The Pamir and Swiss Alps are also popular among the foreign tourists to a great extent. The Tibetan Plateau has become on attraction among the wildland trekkers of the world. The journey through rail upto the base of Everest has opened many gates to success in tourism for the Chinese government. But this will pollute and destroy the environment of the whole of Himalayas. The wildlife and flora diversity will certainly be affected by these developments.

Nature tourism has become quite popular among the nations of the world. This has affected the pristine wildlands where the tourists flock in large numbers. In this way some beautiful landscapes in the world have been destroyed permanently. For example, Costa Rica, Ecuador, Nepal, Kenya, Madagascar and Antarctica is doing well in nature tourism but several parts of their scenic lands have been destroyed in the past one decade Nature Tourism has brought peace and prosperity in some acres of the world. When there is economic development there is a great social change. A change through prosperity. Tourism provides great economic build up and transformation in social, educational and political areas. This economic transformation provides new dimensions of development and progress in life. The great economic and social change of Spain and France is because of tourism development in those countries. The prosperity through tourism is quick and multipurpose. We can achieve this through encouraging nature tourism in the country.

Acronyms

ATP	Asian Tiger Project
AEP	Asian Elephant Project
AACL	Association of Alpine Clubs of India
AOS	American Orchid Society
AWA	American Wilderness Alliance
AWF	African Wildlife Foundation,
IPA	Important Plant Areas
IBA	Important Bird Areas
ISGVI	International Society Global Villages of India
ISWFAP	International Society For Wildflowers and Alpine plants, India
IWA	International Wilderness Association India
IDS	Institute of Development Studies, UK
IWL	International Wilderness Leadership, USA
FFI	Fauna and Flora International, UK
ACIAR	Australian Council for International Agricultural Research
ACORD	Agency Cooperation Research and Development
ADRAO	Association de Development du d' Afrique Quest (WARDA)
AERDD	Agricultural Extension and Rural Development Department (UK)
AGRITEX	Government of Zimbabwe Agricultural Extension Service
ASARECA	Association for Strengthening Agricultural Research in Eastern and Central Africa
AWF	African Wildlife Foundation

BAIF	Bharatiya Agro-Industries Foundation
BIRD	BAIF Institute for Rural Development (India)
BRAC	Bangladesh Rural Advencement Committee
CABI	Commonwealth Agricultural Research and Development Institute
CABUNGO	Capacity Building Unit for NGOs
CARDI	Caribbean Agricultural Research and Development Institute
CATIE	Research and Training Center for Tropical Agronomy (Costa Rica)
CAZRI	Central Arid Zone Research Institute
CECAT	China-EU Centre for Agricultural Technology
CDRN	Community Development Resource Network (Uganda)
CIAT	International Center for Tropical Agriculture
CIKARD	Center for Indigenous Knowledge for Agricultural and Rural Development (USA)
CIMMYT	International Center for the Improvement of Maize and Wheat
CIRAD	Center for International Cooperation in Agricultural Development Research (France)
CTA	Technical Center For Agricultural and Rural Corporation (The Netherlands)
DANIDA	Danish International Development Assistance
DARSHN	Development Action through Self Help Network (India)
DFID	Department for International Development (UK)
DRN	Development Researchers' Network
DSE	Development Researches Network
ECDPM	European Center for Development Policy Management
ETC	Educational Training consultants (The Netherlands)

FADO	Flemish Organisation for Assistance in Development
FAO	United Nations Food and Agriculture Organisation
FCO	Foreign and Commonwealth Office (UK)
FINNIDA	Finnish Development Agency
GRET	Group for Technological Research (France)
GTZ	German Agency for Technical Cooperation
IARI	Indian Agricultural Research Institute
ICAFDA	International Centre for Agricultural Research in Dry Areas
ICIMOD	International Center for Integrated Mountain Development
ICLARM	International Center for Living Aquatic Resources Management (Philippines)
GHF	Greenland Heritage Foundation
TWS	The Wilderness Society USA
NCWFR	National Commission For Wild Flower Research
NEWFS	New England Wildflower Society
NWFRC	New England Wildflower Research Center
PCA	Predator Conservation Alliance
WAW	Wild Alabama Wilderness
ICRAF	International Center for Research in Agroforestry
ECRISAT	International Center for Research in the Semi-Arid Tropics
IDES	Interface Development Interventions
IDPM	Institute Development Policy and Management (UK)
IDRC	International Development Research Council (Canada)
IGADD	Inter Governmental Authority on Drought and Development
IGFRI	Indian Grassland and Fodder Research Institute

IIED	International Institute for Environment and Development (UK)
IIMI	International Institute for Environment Institute (Sri Lanka)
IIRR	International Institute of Rural Reconstruction (Philippines)
IITA	International Institute of Tropical Agriculture (Nigeria)
ILEIA	Information Center for Low External Input Agriculture (The Netherlands)
ILRI	International Livestock Research Institute
INRA	National Institute for Agronomic Research (France)
IRMA	Institute of Rural Management
IRRI	International Rice Research Institute
ISNAR	International Center for Low external Input Agriculture (The Netherlands)
ITDG	Intermediate Technology Development Group (UK)
IUCN	World Conservation Union
JIVC	Japan International Volunteer Center
KIT	Royal Tropical Institute (The Netherlands)
KRIBHCO	Krishak Bharati Cooperative Ltd. (India)
MARDI	Malaysian Research and Development Institute
NARO	National Agricultural Research Organisation (Uganda)
NCAP	National Center for Agricultural Economy and Policy Research
NORAGRIC	Norwegian Center of International Agricultural Development
NRI	Natural Resources Institute (UK)
ODI	Overseas Development Institute (UK)
RIMISP	International Network for Methodology and research Production Systems (Chile)

SIDA	Swedish International Development Cooperation Agency
UNDP	United Nations Development Programme
USAID	United States Agency for International Development
WARDA	West Africa Rice Development Association
WARF	West Africa Rural Foundation
WWF	World Wide Fund of Nature
WFPS	Wild Flowers Preservation Society. USA
WEA	Wilderness Education Association USA
FOW	Friends of Wilderness
IWL	International Wilderness Leadership
WSL	Wilderness Survival League
WTY	Wilderness Trek for Youth
WUEA	Wilderness Use Education Association
WIW	Women in the Wilderness
WHC	Wild Heritage Campaign
WTU	Wild Things Unlimited
UNEP	United Nations Environment Programme, New Delhi
UNU	United Nations University, Tokyo, Japan
ECDO	Eco System Development Organisation, Nigeria
PADP	Plateau Agriculture Development Project, Nigeria
WPRPL	Woodville Palace Resorts Private Limited, Shimla, India
WAO	Woodville Apple Orchards, Nerwa, HP, India

References

1. Wildlife and Eco-Tourism, Taj Rawat, Paryavaran Magazine, Ministry of Environment and Forestry.
2. American Herbal News Bulletin USA.
3. The Botanical Market Place, Robert D'McCaleb, USA.
4. The Wilderness Society Bulletin, USA.
5. Journal of Non-Timber Forest products Vol. 4,1997, Dehradun.
6. Ethnobotanical Studies, Indian Journal of Forestry, Dehradun
7. Glimpes of Indian Ethnobotany, S.K.Jain, IBH, New Delhi.
8. Evolution of Crop Plants, Simmonds, NW, Longman London.
9. Environment of The Himalayas, Taj Rawat (In Press).
10. Eco Forum, Nairobi, Kenya.
11. Wilderness Management in the Mountains, Taj Rawat Encology July, 1997.
12. The Beauty of Orchids, Taj Rawat, Hindustan Times, April 28,96
13. Japanese Journal of Himalayan Botany, Univ. of Tokyo.
14. Herb Products, American Herbs Association, CA, USA.
15. The Orchids, American Orchid Society FI, USA.
16. Fauna and Flora International Cambridge, UK.
17. Pahari-Kheti Bari-Medicinal Plants, G.B.P. University Complex, Ranichauri, Tehri, UP.
18. The Valley of Gods and Goddesses Taj Rawat, (Press)
19. Exploring the High Mountain Pastures Taj Rawat, (Press)
20. Lindleyana, American Orchid Society 1997.

21. The Ecologist, UK.
18. Flora: New Threat, Raj Chengappa, India Today, May 31, 1993.
19. Conservation of Orchid Forests of Dehradun, National Herald 1996, Taj Rawat.
20. Lindleyana, American Orchid Society 1997.
21. The Ecologist, UK.
22. Science, AAAS. USA.
23. Nature Resources, UNESCO, Paris France.
24. Environment Conservation, Univ, New Castle, U.K.
25. Indian Journal of Botany, ICSR, New Delhi.
26. Medicinal Plants of the Grahwal Hills, Taj Rawat (Press)
27. Farm Radio Bulletins, Developing Countries Farm Radio Network, Canada.
28. The Great American Wilderness, WWF - 1997.
29. Hamara Paryavaran, Taj Rawat Takshshila Publishing House New Delhi.
30. Mountain Tourism and Range Land Management, ICIMOD, Kathmandu, Nepal.
31. Oryx, Fauna and Flora International, U.K.
32. The Importance of Tibetan Plateau, Environment of the Himalayas by Taj Rawat, New Delhi.
33. Wild life Habitat Enhancement Council, Silver Springs, MD, USA.
34. Wilderness Medical Society, CA, USA.
35. Wildernes Watch, WI, USA.
36. Wilderness Education Association, New York, USA.
37. Rocky Mountain Center for Botanical Studies, Boulder Co., USA.
38. Adventure Education, U.K.
39. Wilderness Society, Washington DC, USA.
40. Wildlife Harvest Magazine, Gooselake, IA, USA.
41. Natural History Magazine, NY, USA.

42. International Wilderness Association, Woodville Resorts, Shimla.
43. Grass land Heritage Foundation, USA.
44. The Wild Foundation, CA, USA.
45. International Society For Mountain Studies and Research, New Delhi
46. International Society For Global Village of India, New Delhi.
47. The Mountaineers, WA, USA.
48. Falcon Publishing Inc. MT, USA.
49. Nomad Mountain Publications UK.
50. The Wilderness Society, USA.
51. The Woodville Palace Resorts Pvt. Ltd., Shimla, H.P. India.
52. The Woodville Orchards, Nerwa, H.P., India
53. Geography of Tourism and Recreation Michael Hill Stephen J. Page Routledge, UK
54. Encyclopedia of Eco - Tourism, weaver, Cabi-UK
55. Managing Environment For Leisure And Recreation, Broad hurst, UK
56. Eco-Tourism in Less Developed World, Weaver, Cabi UK
57. Tourism in Western Europe, Cabi, UK
58. Wilderness Management and Eco-Tourism: Taj Rawat, Sunshine, New Delhi.
59. Exploring The High Mountain Wilderness: Taj Rawat, (Press) New Delhi.
60. Vishwa Paryavaran: Ek Adhyayan, Taj Rawat, Praveen Prakashan New Delhi.
61. Paryavaran Paryatan Evam Lok Sanskriti, Taj Rawat, New Academic Publishers.
62. Paryatan Bazar, Sanchar Evan Vigyapan Prabandhan, Taj Rawat
63. Paryaravan Paryatan Evam Prabandhan, Taj Rawat, Takshshila.
64. Progressing Tourism Research Bill Faulkner-Viva Books
65. Shopping Tourism: Daldon Timothy-Viva

—

66. Recreational Tourism: ChisRyan-Viva Books
67. National Area Tourism: Newsome: Moare and Douling
68. Tourism and Employment: Sharplley Telfer
69. Tourism and Employment: Riley, Ladkin, Szivas
70. Tourism, Globalization and Cultural Change, Donald Mcleod
71. Tourism Marketing: Fyall and Garrod
72. Tourism, Recreation and Climate Change. Hall and Higham
73. Sport Tourism: Ratchei and Adain
74. Sport Tourism Development. Hinch and Higham
75. Tourism Mobility and Second Home : Hall and Muller
76. Tourism Development: Issues for Vulnerable Industry
77. Nature based Tourism in Peripheral Areas. Hall and Boyd
78. Holidays and Calebration: Mathen Denni
79. Encyclopaedia of Earth Science
80. Encylopaedia of Environmental Studies. Ashworth/ Lihle
81. Encyelopaedia of World Geography. Rm Mccou
82. Encyelopaedia of Biology. Rithner and Mcabe
83. Encyelopaedia of Blizzards: Micheel Alkmby
84. Sustainable Tourism. Lasly France: Earthscan
85. The Global Enviroment Vig and Axelord
85. Global Action for Bio-diversity: Twnethy Swanson
87. Global Environment; outlook, UNEP
88. The Root Causes of Biodiversity loss Wood and Many Earthen
89. The Basis of Rural Tourism : International Perspectives. J. Page D. Getz
90. Community, Ecology and Environment VK Prabhakar
91. Across the Peaks and Passes in Garhwal Himalaya : H. Kapadia.
92. Across The Himalayan Gap : An Indian Quest for Understanding China/Tan Chung

93. Agricultural Modernisation in Eastern Himalayas : MC Behra
94. Alpine Plants of Western Himalayas C.M. Sharma
95. Altai Himalaya : Travel Diary : N. Roerich
96. Bio-diversity and Environment A. Kumar
97. Bio-diversity social and Ecological Perspective.
98. Bio-diversity and its conservation in India S.S. Negi
99. British Kumaon Garhwal : R.S. Tolia
100. Central Asia and Tibet : Sven Hedin
101. Central Asia and Kashmir Himalaya : P. Kachroo
102. Aspects of Geology and Environment of the Himalaya : Charu Pant, Arun Sharma
103. Comprehensive Ecological Botanical Survey of the Grasses : A.B. Chaudhuri.
104. Citadel of Ice Dakshin Gangotri : The First Indian Wintering in Antarctica : Satya S. Sharma.
105. Chamba Himalaya : Amazing land, Unique Culture : R. Bharati
106. Ecological Crisis is the Himalayas S.K. Chadha
107. Ecological Impact of Apple Cultivation in the Himalaya Vir Singh.
108. Ecology, Tribals and Rural Development
109. Himalayas Biodiversity : Conservation Strategies U. Dhar
110. Himalayan Desert : (Tibet, Ladakh, Lahaul, Spiti, Mustang.
111. Nina Rao High Pasturelands of Ladakh Himalaya, Prem Singh Jeena
112. Himalaya : Environment, Resources and Development NK Shah
113. Himalayan Kingdom : Roof of the World Jon Burbank
114. Himalayas Misteries : Ganesh Saili.
115. Trekking in the Himalaya : Harshpat Singh
116. Trans Himalaya Discoveries and Adventures : Sven Hedin

Index

❑❑❑